FOREWORD BY DR. SCOTT POLAND

TEENS WITH TENACITY

Helping teens build the tenacity
needed to succeed in life

Glenn Girls Press
545 ½ Lighthouse Avenue
Pacific Grove, CA 93950

Cataloging-in-Publication Data is on file at the Library of Congress

Paperback ISBN: 979-8-9882932-0-0
eBook ISBN: 979-8-9882932-1-7
Hardcover ISBN: 979-8-9882932-2-4
Audio ISBN: 979-8-9882932-9-3

First Paperback Edition, March 2024
White Page Paperback Edition (2nd), May 2024
First Ebook Edition, March 2024

Printed in the United States of America

For information, contact:
www.kathyespinoza.com
kathy@kathyespinoza.com

FOREWORD BY DR. SCOTT POLAND

TEENS WITH TENACITY

Helping teens build the tenacity needed to succeed in life

KATHY ESPINOZA

JACQUELYN RATHBUN

CHRISTOPHER ESPINOZA

Glenn Girls Press | Monterey

Table of Contents

~ Dedication ~

This book is dedicated to my husband of 44 years, my high school sweetheart. I thank him for always coming home to the 'house of the crazies.' Thank you for your tenacity in putting up with the demands of the job for 41 years, which enabled me to get the help our children needed to be successful.

I'm also dedicating the book to my parents, who instilled the concept of tenacity in me from an early age.

~ A Letter from the Author ~

In a perfect world, a child is born into a perfect family with loving parents who idolize that child and spend their lives trying to make them happy. These parents make sure their child is safe, healthy and has everything they need to be successful in life.

In the real world, we all land into a family that is less than perfect. We may only have one parent to care for us. We may have no parent—only a guardian or a foster family to care for us. We may have so many siblings that our needs are just one of the many. We may feel like we are nothing special but just another burden on a family that is barely making it.

Life happens. Problems happen to everyone, and some are worse than others. These problems impact who we are, who we become and how we cope with what is thrown at us. Our ability (or inability) to handle these events and challenges determines our future.

There are some teens you will read about in this book who have horrific things happen in their lives, but they come out on top. On the other hand, there are teens who experience unimaginable events and choose to find comfort in drugs, gangs, and alcohol.

What is the difference?

Tenacity.

Tenacity is the ability to never give up. Tenacity allows us to believe there is something better. It gives us the strength to overcome those challenges that constantly beat us down. Tenacity gives us the grit to take a deep breath and step forward—even when we don't want to.

This book is for you. It's for anyone who was born into a less than perfect world. It's for teens who struggle with family issues, grades, peer pressures and life in general

It is my sincere hope that you will take the skills found in this book and use tenacity to become the person you want to be. Just believe that it is possible to achieve your dreams and handle what comes at you, no matter how imperfect your life may have started out.

XO, Kathy

~ Foreword by Dr. Scott Poland ~

It is my great pleasure to provide a foreword for this excellent book for teenagers illustrating the importance of tenacity. Having worked with school students for over 40 years, I've responded to 17 school shootings and many youth suicide point clusters and have developed a great deal of expertise in crisis intervention and served on many national crisis teams. I've devoted a large part of my career as a licensed psychologist to youth suicide prevention.

I'm extremely aware of how challenging it is to be a teen in today's world. In fact, the U.S. Surgeon General recently put out advisories of which the first emphasized the need to seize the moment and promote mental health for young people.

The second advisory addressed the potential dangers of screen time and social media on our youth.

To summarize what the U.S. Surgeon General stressed in just one sentence: Social media results in our youth feeling that they are not smart enough, not rich enough and not good enough.

There is a great deal of competition and pressure on our teens. Add that to the many United States and world issues that affect them!

Sadly, suicide is now the second leading cause of death for teenagers.

This book by Kathy Espinoza provides teens with important tools they can utilize to manage the stress in their lives and move with tenacity towards their goals.

We all wish that every teen lived in a stable home and was shown unconditional love by their caregivers, but that is not always the case. Their struggle and the need for tenacity is well articulated through this book's numerous vignettes that capture the many adverse experiences that teens face. Valuable questions are provided through homework assignments covering many important areas such as goal setting, self-care, and managing stress.

During the pandemic, I was asked to create virtual sessions for students, school staff, and parents to manage stress. I developed a four-point model called C.A.L.M. Every letter stood for a key concept and these concepts are all emphasized in this book.

The C focuses on what we can Control, which is only our reaction to what's happening.

The A stands for being Alert to behavioral and emotional changes that we're experiencing and also for making ourselves Available to our family and friends.

The L stands for truly Listening to our friends and family. As a psychologist, two words that I rarely use are, "I understand." We cannot really understand unless something like that has happened to us. It is important to truly listen to someone in distress and not to give them a pep-talk or tell them about something we learned when we were experiencing a difficult time.

The L also stands for Limiting screen time and especially the exposure to traumatic events. I like to ask teens if they have ever missed out on some things that they would really like to do because of the amount of time they spend on screens. You'd be surprised how many answer, "Yes."

The M stands for Modeling of optimism and hope for the future. It is important for teens to seek out those people in their lives who are positive and encouraging and to be that person for others. This book provides many activities for teens to reflect on their choices, manage their time and strive for balance in their lives.

I have great hope for the future of our current teens and believe that they will learn important skills by reading this book.

I especially liked the emphasis on volunteering, as I have often found that the only way a teen can truly find themselves is through service to other people.

Kathy has done a brilliant job describing through vignettes the incredible array of challenges that teens face and has provided examples of them receiving help from school mental health professionals. I am a strong believer that every teen needs to have at least one go-to trusted adult.

This book contains many excellent recommendations for teens but a very important one that is highlighted is to get proper rest as that is often the key to managing adversities.

I recommend this book highly as it captures the many challenges teens face and provides them with very practical strategies on how to respond with tenacity. It is important for teens themselves and the adults in their lives to never give up. Everything rarely goes perfectly for teens, and tenacity is important!

Dr. Scott Poland, Licensed Psychologist

National Crisis Responder,

Psychology Professor and Director of the Suicide and Violence

Prevention Office, NSU Florida, Fort Lauderdale, Florida

Chapter 1

JOSEPHINA'S STORY

I got out of work at the local pizza place last night at 10 p.m. After staying up until 12 a.m. to finish all of my homework, I woke up at 5 a.m. to get my three younger brothers and sisters ready for school.

They fought me the entire time, and I had no strength or patience for their behavior. I snapped at them that I didn't want to wake up either. But here I am, not just waking myself up but three ungrateful younger siblings, too.

I dress them, comb their hair, make them breakfast, and pack their lunches. I clean the dishes and the kitchen countertops while they moan and groan that it is too early, and they don't want to go to school. I help them find their homework and chrome books, get them in their backpacks and hurry them out the door.

Why am I, the 15-year-old, doing what most parents should be doing?

My dad works all night on the night shift. He is exhausted when he comes home and goes right to sleep. My mom works the early morning shift at her job. Then she goes to a second job in the afternoon. Otherwise, the bills go unpaid.

It's not fair, and I'm mad that I have to be the one to take care of not only myself but three younger siblings who all think I'm a tyrant. I'm not their parent, but I may as well be.

I hear my mom crying herself to sleep every night. She is so overwhelmed and stressed. My dad takes out his frustration and anger from his job on all of us. When he is tired or has a bad day at work, he fights with my mom, and they fight constantly.

My siblings crawl into my bed whenever our parents are fighting in the middle of the night. I hug them close and put on some quiet, comforting music for them so they can try to sleep. I love my mom dearly, and she is absolutely everything to me. That's why I do what she asks me to do every day, without complaining.

But I'm tired.

I feel like I have to be a 2nd mom to these three little ones. I'm taking hard classes at high school that come with a lot of homework. I have a part-time job to help our family with money and bills.

Lately, I'll admit, I've been a little short with everyone. I can't control my frustration and anger. I feel like no one understands what I'm going through. What hurts most is that they probably don't care.

I pile all three kids in the car with me, a 15-year-old without a license, and drive them to school. I drop off two at the elementary school, one at the middle school, and finally, I drive to my high school.

I don't have a license because we can't afford for me to go to driver's ed classes. My parents can't take us to school because they are asleep or at work, and going on the bus would take several hours. So, here I am, at 15, risking it all to make sure my family can function day in and day out.

Today, my siblings were extra tired. Mom and Dad were up late arguing and none of us kids got much sleep. It took forever to wake them up and get them ready. But we did it and made it to school.

I got everyone there on time, barely, but now I'm late. I park and run to my 1st-period class ten minutes late. My teacher rolls her eyes at me when I walk in.

"Late again, I see…" she hisses at me.

She is already on my last nerve. My stomach is in a knot, and I feel like I'm ready to explode. I just give her a glare and take my seat. I have no idea what anyone is doing. I missed the instructions. I raise my hand and ask what we are doing.

My teacher gives me an attitude and says, "Maybe if you woke up earlier and tried to be more responsible, then you would be here on time and know what we are doing."

The class laughs at this. My face turns red.

She has absolutely no idea how responsible I am. I want to scream, "I'm a teen who's running my entire household! What I've already done this morning would take you a week to get done. I don't need to be minimized or laughed at."

I can feel the rage coming up, and I yell at her, "You don't f**king know what you are talking about! You don't know a damn thing about me!"

The teacher glares at me and yells back, "How DARE you be so disrespectful?!" She calls for a campo.

I tell her, "I don't f**king care! I don't want to be here anyway!" She writes me a referral and sends me to the office.

While I wait to talk to the assistant principal in the main office, I am steaming. She doesn't know anything. I'm sooo damn tired. I feel hot tears come down my cheeks. My dad is going to whoop me. He is going to tell me that I have to control myself and respect my teachers. He doesn't even respect my mom. He yells at her, calls her names, and screams all night long.

That teacher had NO right to call me irresponsible. She doesn't know my life or what I'm up against.

The assistant principal calls me in, and I'm ready to fight and stand up for myself. I go into his office and yell, "I'm BIG mad. That b**ch doesn't even know me! She doesn't know what I go through every day! She humiliated me. Everyone laughed at me! I HATE her!"

The assistant principal sees I'm very upset. He can tell that there is more going on…something I'm not telling him. He tells me that he sees I'm going through a lot. He is going to send me to the counselor's office today, but he does have to give me a consequence for my actions. No matter what I'm going through, he tells me I cannot take it out on other people, even when they test my patience.

I'm annoyed, but I take my punishment (a class suspension for two days) and go to the counselor's office. No one cares. No one really sees me. No one understands the pressure I'm under.

I hate this.

I hate all of this. I just want to scream with rage. Nothing I do is ever enough. What can a counselor do to heal all my frustration, anger, and resentment? I walk into the counselor's office and sit…

NEWS FLASH: TEENS DO HAVE STRESS!

You even have more stress than your parents had when they were teens. There are a lot of young people going through the same problems and pressures that you are going through. Most are not sure how to handle all that inner turmoil.

Teens experience anger, fear, and happiness, sometimes all within moments. Emotions are all over the place, like a swinging pendulum. Not sure what to do with all that emotion, it's easy to act out on impulse. Teens may try to control their circumstances or control other people to get what they want.

You will learn in this book that you can't control what happens in life. You can only control <u>how you react</u> to what happens in life.

LIFE IS A JUGGLING ACT

Adults and teens are juggling a lot of stressballs (issues) in their lives. Everyone has stressballs in the air that they are trying to keep balanced, without letting any one of them drop. Parents are juggling jobs, their house, paying the bills, buying groceries, getting kids clothed, fed, and to school.

But what about teens? Do teenagers have stress? Are they trying to juggle homework, friends, enemies, peer pressure, social media, bullying? YES! Teens have a lot going on, but no one seems to notice…or care.

Here are some comments you may hear:

"Oh, you think you have stress…honey, just wait until you are my age."

"What do you have to worry about?"

"Every day is Christmas for a kid."

Your stress is real. Your problems in life are significant. Every challenge you face, every single day, matters. These challenges can affect your mood, your energy and your personality.

Stress is not just a word used by adults. Parents and adults are not the only ones who have to deal with real-life problems. They are not the only ones who go to bed worried. They are not the only ones who feel fear, pain and worry.

THINK ABOUT IT:

I'd like you to think about all you are trying to juggle. What are the stressballs you are collecting? What went wrong today?

Who is mad at me? Sports? Parents getting a divorce? Brothers? Sisters? Parent's health? Family finances? Grandparents getting older? Are you raising your siblings?

What do you want to do with your life? College? Find a trade? Don't you feel tired from carrying around all these stressballs and juggling them in your mind? You go home after school, and it feels so good to escape into your phone. Checking out TikTok: who posted what. Deeper and deeper you go, hour after hour, just to take your mind off the stressballs you are worrying about.

The problem is that sometimes, we take all these stressballs to bed with us. When you try and go to sleep, all those juggling stressballs resurface in your mind. You start thinking about them. You worry about how you will fix them. What are you going to say to that person tomorrow? How will you pass that test? Can you even make it to school on time for once?

Your alarm goes off in the morning, and you start the day tired. Juggling all night long doesn't make for a good night's sleep, which is why you are cranky and sleep-deprived.

My question: Do you **have** to juggle all those stressballs? Are there some that are less important than others? Are you juggling other people's problems?

You decide. Is it worth all that effort to take on every problem and worry about it all night? If it's your friend's problem, let your friend worry about it. If you got a bad grade on a test, take accountability and decide to do the make-up work.

You are the only one who can choose to take on those stressballs that you are trying to juggle. Decide today, is this problem one I want to take to bed and worry about all night? If it's not, let it go. Each time it creeps back into your head, picture a big STOP sign and say, "NO!" out loud. Find another thought to dwell on, but don't allow that issue to become a stressball you juggle all night.

TOO MANY STRESSBALLS IN THE AIR

Why is teen stress today so different from when your parents were teens? It's called "Sandwich Stress." As a teenager, you are caught in the middle between your parents' needs and your own. Here is a better way to explain "Sandwich Stress":

✓ Working parents. Years ago, one parent stayed home while the other one worked. Today, there's a good chance that both parents are working.

✓ Raising your siblings. With both parents working one (or in some cases two or three) jobs, who does that leave to clean the house, cook dinner, help the siblings get their homework done? You.

✓ Not enough time. After you finish helping your parents, there isn't enough time to get your homework done and have a social life. You feel trapped between being a young adult and having a teenage life. This makes you feel angry and resentful.

THINK ABOUT IT:

How do you get back to feeling balanced from being in the Sandwich Stress zone? You have every right to feel stressed because you have a lot of stressballs you are trying to juggle. Your parents are juggling as fast as they can, but so are you.

There are some coping skills you can learn to handle all this pressure and built-up frustration. These skills can make juggling those stressballs more manageable. Maybe even help keep you out of the principal's office.

To understand how these coping skills can help you handle day-to-day stressors faced, let's look at three factors:

1. Start with knowing and acknowledging what stresses you out.
2. Discover how stress affects you mentally and physically.
3. Find out what to do about all this stress.

WHAT IS IT THAT STRESSES ME OUT?

Imagine you wake up and feel pretty good. You got all your homework done and you are on time, for once. You are at a 1 on a scale of 1 to 5 (a 5 is where you have blown it: You lash out at your teacher, call your friend a name, cuss and swear, lose control and are now heading down to the principal's office).

What is it in life that takes you from a 1…all the way to a 5? What takes you "over the edge" mentally and emotionally? What takes it from being a good day to an awful day? Is it a bad hair day? Or you tried on five shirts and still feel crappy? Maybe someone posted something about you on social media.

What is it that you are feeling when you know you've gone from a 1 to a 5, and now it's a miserable day? Your body gives you signs that tell the world that you are losing control and having a bad day. It is important to know the signs your body gives you.

THINK ABOUT IT:

What are the signs that your **parents** are tapped out? When they are definitely at a 5? How do they show that they are at their limit? Do they scream and shout? Do they bark out orders, one after another? What do they do, that tells you to "lay low" and don't make them any angrier?

What are the signs that your **friends** are tapped out? When they are definitely at a 5? How do your friends show that they are having a horrible day? What signals do they have? Do they get really loud or mad at everything? Do they cross their arms and sulk? Do they get quiet and ignore you?

What do **YOU** do to show when **you** are tapped out? What are your signs that show when you are getting overwhelmed? Book reports are due, college essays, applications, tests… What signals do you show that let everyone know you are going from that 1 to a 5 on the panic scale?

Some teens shut down when they feel stressed. Some teens tend to feel unmotivated or talk negatively to themselves. They say, "I can't do this homework… I'm just stupid… I'll never amount to anything…"

Some teens become mentally exhausted from carrying around all the stressballs and worrying day and night. All they want to do is sleep. Sleep is an "escape." You need to learn to cope with what comes at you in life—not escape it—because it will still be there when you wake up.

It's important to recognize these signs because how can you fix it, if you can't recognize when it's happening?

WHY DO WE EVEN CARE ABOUT STRESS?

Stress affects your body down to the cellular level. It can make you age and look older. Take President Obama. When he first became President, he had black hair. After 8 years of being President, his hair had turned white!

Of course, not all stress is harmful.

There is "good stress" and "bad stress."

Look at your parent's wedding photo. Their wedding day was filled with good stress. There was a lot to do and lots of planning, but overall, it was a fun day. Another example is prom. Prom is fun, but it's stressful to get everything planned and ready: the dress, the tux, the ride, the tickets, the dinner.

Good stress is okay because you are working towards something. It has an end, and if well planned, everyone had a good time.

Bad stress is something that goes on forever. You worry about it day and night. You juggle the stressballs. Your body is tense. You feel anger and anxiety. It's like a leaky faucet that just drips, drips, drips. It doesn't end. It goes on day and night. Bad stress affects your health. It affects your attitude and the person you are.

When you spend all day and night thinking, *I should have… I could have… I would have…*, it will change your body.

Everyone's body reacts to stress in different ways.

For a lot of people, it feels like they can't take in a full breath. For others, their heart starts to pound. They can feel their heart beating in their ears. Some people feel their neck and face getting warm. Some begin to sweat.

These are just a few of the signs that your body is experiencing stress. Your body is reacting to all the problems, pressures and issues you've encountered today.

SO, WHAT DO I DO WITH ALL THIS STRESS?

It's important to learn how to handle stress **when you first start feeling it** in your body. This will help you to develop good coping strategies for life. It all begins with understanding stress.

I asked you earlier: What is stress to you? You identified the issues and problems that you are worrying about, all the things that take you from a 1 to a 5, that take you over the edge.

But what is stress exactly? Is it all those events that you juggle in your head, day and night? It is your mom, dad, teacher, brother, sister, traffic getting to school, homework?

Or… Is stress how you **handle** those events?

LET'S TALK ABOUT STRESS

The answer is **not** all the things going wrong all day. The answer is that STRESS is how **you** deal with it. All those things you encounter every day that build up are called "stressors."

There are teens who have a LOT of things go wrong. Only, they don't let it get to them. They take a deep breath and practice of few stress management techniques and keep going.

An earthquake is a good example. In California, we have earthquakes all the time. Most of us shrug our shoulders and say, "It will pass."

What about the teen who just moved here from North Dakota, where they don't have earthquakes? When that same earthquake happens, you will watch them panic and dive under the desk.

In this example, both teens had the same stressor: the earthquake. But they each handled it differently. Stress is like beauty. It's in the eye of the beholder. If you THINK something is stress, your body will react to it as stress and then produce negative signs.

That's what I'm asking you to do…recognize the signs of stress and handle the stressors differently. It starts with changing your perception.

HOMEWORK:

1. What does stress look like to you?

2. How do you feel when stress is coming on?

3. What are your signs that tell the world you are stressed?

4. What stressors can you change your perception about?

SELF-REFLECTION:

It's important to know what signs your body gives you that indicate you are getting stressed. Recognizing when you are getting stressed can actually give you the power to do something about it.

TIPS FOR TEACHERS:

Teachers do not always know what is going on behind the scenes. We do not always know what is happening at home or what our students are mentally and emotionally going through.

When we see a student who is having a meltdown, instead of making them an example for the rest of the class, it's important to take them aside privately. Ask if they are okay. Most of the time they are not okay.

Students have a lot of pent-up anger, stress and frustration. They just don't know how to cope and sometimes take it out on an easy target: a teacher, a friend or another loved one. That person is usually a safe mark who the student knows will forgive them.

If you see a student who is upset, stressed, has tears coming down their face (or brimming in their eyes), is breathing heavily, or is putting their head down trying to escape, pull them aside. Tell them you are there for them if they need anything or want to talk. Usually, this lets them know they are seen. It shows the student that there is someone who cares. This can make a big difference.

It will also help if you let your student know that you will be sending the counselor an email to follow up with them. Tell them the counselor is another safe person who cares. Giving teens room to speak and letting them know we are here for them, allows them to engage in a conversation about their lives.

Teachers play a huge role in identifying students who are in crisis or who need mental health help. We are with our students every day. We see shifts in their moods and behaviors. We can be a solid bridge in getting them help from the counselor, other educators, and even a mental health worker. If our student lets us know what is wrong, we can help them with accommodations. This could be a little extra time on an assignment or tutoring help at lunch or after school. It could be letting the student take or retake a test if they were having a bad day. It could be letting the student see the counselor if they are struggling and need a period to reset.

Bottom line is that it's important for us to be there for our students both academically and emotionally.

COUNSELOR'S THOUGHTS:

I would actively listen to Josephina and understand that she is carrying a tremendous load.

As school counselors, we have the delicate task of helping bridge the gap between the student's personal life and the teacher's expectation for success in their classroom. The student's academic experience does not exist within the vacuum of a teacher's classroom. Their personal life and the experiences that are out of their control will always play a part in their day-to-day success.

We educators like to think we show all of our students the care they need when we work with them. In reality, there are just not enough hours in a school day to give every student the time and understanding they truly need. One of the best things a school can do is proactively work with their educators on developing compassion for these students.

As counselors, we can do this by providing training at a staff in-service on a "Handle with Care" program and its protocols for students like Josephina. The "Handle with Care" program allows the counselors, who are privy to many personal details of a student's family life, to keep other educators in the school informed. Counselors are able to share that the student, their family or loved one is experiencing something beyond their control. This alerts the other educators that it's a very stressful time in their student's life.

However, before disclosing any details about the student's life to other staff, I would first ask Josephina if she feels comfortable with me sharing her situation. Many times, students like Josephina refuse to share that information with adults who they believe don't actually care. This is why "Handle with Care" privacy protocols are important.

If Josephina gives her consent to me, I would set up a time with all her teachers and have a discussion about what's going on. This would allow open dialog on circumstantial accommodations for her success. Could there be deadline extensions for projects? Homework and test prep? Study guide assistance?

Programs like "Handle with Care" remind staff of two important considerations. The student is doing their best under their current situation, and staff should give an extra bit of "Care" until more information is obtained. This information will help teachers pause and reflect before reacting to the student's behavior or lack of participation.

This trauma-informed practice would give teachers the skills they need to realize that their student isn't late because they are lazy or oversleeping. It would help them see that it's the circumstances in the student's life that are directly impacting their ability to arrive on time.

After learning about Josephina's home life, I would try to build rapport with her through scheduled check-ins over the next few weeks. From her comments such as, "No one cares at this school," I would do my best to establish a connection with her, so she could identify me as a safe adult she can trust.

Many times, when a student doesn't feel safe with adults on campus, it is because they don't think the adults have any interest in them as individuals beyond academics. Knowing this would lead me to try to connect Josephina with another adult on campus, so she knows there are other adults who are genuinely interested in her wellbeing.

After learning how difficult and stressful Josephina's mornings are, I would discuss a schedule change with her. We could look into the possibility of switching her 1st period from a core class to an elective or PE. This would give her more time in the morning to handle the family responsibilities without having to stress about the demanding load found in 1st period English, History or Math.

I would also discuss the possibility of making a counseling referral to the district's partnered mental health services for Josephina. This would allow her an opportunity to attend counseling sessions to discuss her tremendous family responsibilities, her sibling and family dynamics, and her own mental health. These services are school-based and wouldn't be an additional financial burden to the family.

JOSEPHINA'S OUTCOME:

Josephina realized that no one could know what she is going through unless she tells them. The counselor reached out to her teachers to let them know what she was up against, and they immediately felt more empathy.

Her teachers worked with her. They gave her more time on assignments to help her get her grades up. If she was tired from lack of sleep, they would let her take the test on a different day when she was more rested.

Her teachers saw her success from these accommodations. They even recommended her for honors classes.

Josephina got to know her teachers very well, and they wrote her excellent letters of recommendation for college. She chose to go to a local four-year state college, as it was cheaper and closer to home than out-of-state universities. That way, she could still help her parents with her siblings. By this time, however, she was able to share that responsibility with her next younger sibling who was old enough to help out more.

Her school counselor helped Josephina get grants (free money) for college. Her family was very low income, so with her high grades in challenging classes, her tuition was paid for. She also received merit scholarships for her grades and for what she accomplished during high school in helping to raise her siblings and work part-time jobs.

Josephina is a glowing example for her siblings to follow in her footsteps. She changed the trajectory of her family by being the first one to attend and graduate from college.

All of Josephina's hard work, dedication, and tenacity paid off.

Chapter 2

SAMIR'S STORY

Football practice just ended, and it's 9 o'clock, so late. I'm tired, but I don't mind. Playing football is the only thing that ever feels good anymore. I take out all my pent-up anger and rage on my opponents on the field. I lay it all out there.

After practice, I come home, eat the quick dinner my mom left for me, shower, and then sit down and look at my mountain of homework.

"I can't," I say to myself. "I'll just wake up early tomorrow and do it. Right now, my body needs rest."

I lie down and take out my phone. A quick jaunt on social media won't hurt, but three hours fly by in the blink of an eye. I turn off my phone, roll over, and go to sleep.

My mom wakes me up for school and is angry…again. She is mad because I am late, again. This woman is always mad at me. I swear she hates me. My dad left us when I was six years old, and she's been angry ever since. After he left, I had to be the man of the house.

I love my mom, but I don't always listen to her. She nags at me constantly. "Samir, help me clean the house… Samir, the dishes need to be done… Samir, take out the trash."

Nag. Nag. Nag.

I'm sick and tired of hearing her whine. Why can't SHE clean the house? I have school and football. I don't have time to clean up after her and me. That's HER job! I don't care if the house is messy. If she cares so much, she can do it alone.

I walk to school because my mom left for her job an hour ago. I get there late as usual and go straight to 1st period. When I walk in, my teacher, Mrs. Rose, looks me up and down. She looks at the clock and rolls her eyes at me. God, she reminds me so much of my mom. She irritates me. She's never happy with me. I can't do anything right. I made it to school, didn't I? I don't even want to be here.

Mrs. Rose says, "Class, take out last night's homework."

I let out a loud groan and ask, "Mrs. Rose, why are you always assigning so much homework? We have other things to do besides homework. Your class is not the only thing that matters!"

She gives me that look that says she's upset with me, and I don't care. This is all HER fault for assigning too much work. I wouldn't have said all that if she hadn't made me so angry.

"I will take this up with your coach later today," she says. "Maybe he can get you to do your work."

I shoot out of my seat and start yelling, "You can't do that! There's NO reason to do that. I didn't do anything to you! Leave my coach out of this!"

I'm fuming. If I lose football, I'll lose everything that matters to me.

I HATE her. This is ALL her fault. I storm out and go to my coach's room.

By the time I get there, it's clear that he has already heard from my teacher. He looks very upset with me.

I immediately go on the offensive and tell him, "I didn't do anything wrong. She's a b**ch! She hates me! She assigns way too much work and has so much attitude. The only reason I popped off was because SHE made me mad! This is all her fault! She blew this waaay out of proportion."

The coach sits me down and says, "We can't have you play in the game this week. Your grades have dropped across the board lately. All of your teachers have emailed me saying you are not doing the work. They can't all be to blame. It seems the common denominator here…is you. At some point, you have to realize this is a 'YOU' problem."

I stare at the ground. I want to yell. I feel the anger rising in my gut. ALL of my teachers have betrayed me. I hate them all! I know yelling at my coach won't do any good because he'll just kick me off the team, so I say, "Fine! I'll get my homework done today. If I get my grades up, will you let me play this week?"

He says, "I'll think about it, but first, you need to control your anger."

I think, like hell, I will. *I plan to give my teachers hell tomorrow.*

I leave my coach's office to head over to 2nd period. When I walk in, Mr. Sanchez tells me the counselor's office has called for me. I ask, "What for?" *Mr. Sanchez doesn't know.*

Oh, great. Mrs. Rose didn't just call my coach. She called the counselor as well. Now I'm super mad. Mrs. Rose thinks she cares about me, but she doesn't because she's failing me. She doesn't care that she's getting me kicked out of this week's football game. She doesn't care that I'm too tired at the end of the day to do her stupid work.

Besides, what can this idiot counselor possibly say to fix any of this? He knows nothing about my life or what I have to deal with!

The counselor opens the door to his office...

IT'S ALL THEIR FAULT!

Having the feeling that everyone around you is on your back can be very normal for teens who are overwhelmed or carry huge responsibilities.

Thinking it's other people's fault gives them a sense of control in a world where it seems they have none.

It's easy to blame the world for everything that goes wrong. Too easy.

This chapter talks about how to deal with overwhelming emotions instead of blaming others for your problems. It gives you tools you can use to bring your body back to that healthy balance between school, home, friends, and family.

HOW DO TEENS TYPICALLY HANDLE STRESS?

Anger is one way of showing the world you are stressed. You've seen how Samir uses anger in an (ineffective) effort to cope with the world around him. Eating comfort foods and having distorted thinking patterns are two other responses to stress.

Let's talk about what happens when you handle stress by getting angry.

You can see anger on the road when driving. Maybe someone cuts you off in your car. Maybe they are driving too close behind you. You feel your heart starting to race. You start breathing faster.

This anger building up is called road rage. (Hopefully, you've never experienced it while driving.)

You start yelling at the other driver. You might honk or give them the finger.

You think, *I'll show him! How dare he cut me off!*

All this rage just keeps coming up from inside you. You speed up to follow the guy. You tailgate his car too closely. Before you know it, he slams on his brakes, and you hit him.

Let's look at rage at school. Someone bumps you in the hall. Maybe it was an accident, but you don't stop long enough to find out. Your heart is pounding, your stomach is clenching, and *BAM!* You respond with anger and rage.

Of course, you've also seen Samir's anger. You've seen him lash out at his teacher, risking the thing he loves most: football.

Usually, before the anger, you get a couple of warning signs. You start to feel anxiety. Your stomach clenches up. Your heart races or your cheeks get warm. Then, anger follows.

This is a very common reaction to being overwhelmed with stress. And it's okay to be angry. ***The problem is when you ACT on that anger—when you allow yourself to be impulsive.*** No time to think about it, you just feel the anger building up, and you lash out on impulse.

Hear this well: It's okay to feel anger; it's NOT okay to act out on that anger. Giving in to impulsive anger is not a good response when you are going from a 1 to a 5 on that escalating stress scale!

My goal with stress management and teen tenacity is to help you discover tools to calm that anger down. This chapter shows you how to "think through" a situation, rather than impulsively reacting to it in a fit of rage.

THE 4 STRESS FOODS

Now let's talk about what happens when you handle stress by eating your feelings.

A lot of teens (and adults, for that matter) start looking for something to eat when they begin feeling anxious and worried. It is called stress eating. Do you do that? Did you know there are four foods in particular that people look for when they start to feel stress?

Chocolate. Chocolate is the number one stress food. It makes us feel good. It releases all kinds of good chemicals in our brains and makes us giddy, like everything is going to be okay. But then there is the sugar crash that happens about an hour later. You find yourself with a bad case of the moody blues and can't understand why. You are short and snippy with your friends and teachers.

Ice Cream. With lots of sprinkles, chocolate sauce and whipped cream. Like chocolate, ice cream is a quick way to feel better. But again, the sugar crash that follows isn't worth it. The constant up-and-down rollercoaster with sugar makes you moody and miserable.

Chips and Salsa. Salty and spicy…the spicier the better. Teens like to "nibble, nibble here; nibble, nibble there" when they feel stressed. It's nice to have crunchy chips next to you when you are doing your homework.

Pizza. Hot or cold…for breakfast, lunch or dinner. Always delicious but not always a good choice when you have anxiety and worry. Pizza puts on weight, which can affect your self-esteem.

Food can be soothing. It comforts us, but stress eating is not a good strategy for managing stress. Remember COVID? That was a stressful time. School was canceled. Everyone had to stay home and learn. People were sick and dying.

Across America, the average weight gain during COVID was twenty-nine pounds! That's a whole preschooler!

Now, the twenty-nine-pound COVID weight gain may not have applied to many teens, but you won't be a teenager with a high metabolism that can burn extra food off forever. Once you enter your 20s, your metabolism slows down, and managing your weight becomes harder.

Remember, reaching for food when you are stressed is not a healthy way to handle life. Try eating crunchy foods like carrots or rice cakes instead of chips. Limit your pizza, chocolate and ice cream intake.

Teen tenacity is about finding skills to handle stress in healthy ways so that you develop solid coping skills you can take into adulthood.

DISTORTED THINKING PATTERNS

What happens when you handle stress with distorted thinking patterns? This begins with overthinking the stressful situation. Overthinking creates weird thoughts (distorted thinking patterns).

My friends hate me.
Everyone thinks I'm stupid.
No one likes me.

Well, this is just not true. Your parents like you. Your brothers and sisters like you. Your friends (if they are real friends) like you.

Other thoughts you may find yourself going to: *I'll never make it to college… I'll never be anything special… I'll be fat and ugly forever…*

Know that these weird thoughts are being driven by stress. Just knowing that does two things for you:

1. It shows you can learn to manage your stress.

2. It takes away the power behind these distorted thinking patterns.

Recognize the signs of being stressed. You are thinking weird thoughts and overthinking every situation. You are lashing out at people. You are feeling moody. You grab chocolate to comfort yourself.

Know that these thoughts and behaviors are your body's way of telling you that you are stressed. Don't take it out on your body or those around you.

There are better ways to handle stress! Instead, use the tools in this book, tools that can get you through the moment.

STRESS MANAGEMENT 101

What do you do when you start feeling those signs and symptoms that tell you that you're getting stressed? What do you do when you feel like you are going from a 1 to a 5 on that stress scale? How do you bring yourself back down and handle it?

1

FIRST, ASK YOURSELF:

"CAN I CONTROL THIS SITUATION?"

Example. My teacher just assigned a book report that is due on Friday. I also have a lab due, a paper to write for another class and an exam to study for. I only have so much time! I feel my heart rate going up, my chest is tight and my stomach hurts. What am I going to do? How will I handle all this?

Control: Ask yourself, "Can I control my teachers?"

The answer is no.

Good time management can help here.

Example. You get home from a long day at school and find the note your mom left for you that has eight chores listed for you to do before she gets home. "Wash the dishes, clean your room, help your sister with her homework, then start dinner, then …"

You feel your heart start racing, it's hard to breathe, your ears are warm, and you feel like you are under water.

Control: Ask yourself, "Can I control my mom?"

The answer is no.

Your mom is a person too, and she needs your help. Your mom may give you a lot to do at home. She may come home upset because she has been dealing with a lot today, too. You cannot control your mom, only yourself and how you handle problems.

2

SECOND, CHANGE THE WAY
YOU LOOK AT WHAT IS BOTHERING YOU.

Remember the earthquake from Chapter 1 where the California teen rides the roll while the teen from North Dakota dives under the table, panicked? It's all in how you look at the situation.

The right perspective gives you the tools to handle problems that come your way.

YOUR UGLY TEN

What is the worst thing you have ever lived through in your life? Something you would never, ever want to go through again? It was that bad. Maybe it was when your parents got divorced or when your grandma died. Perhaps it was last summer when your brother died in a car accident.

What is your worst life event?

Now picture a ruler. This ruler will serve as your **scale of 1 to 10** on the crummiest things to ever go wrong in your life.

You now know what a 10 looks like on this ruler scale. It's that ugly, horrible time in life. **That's your 10.** Maybe mom or dad died, or maybe it's when your boyfriend or girlfriend broke up with you. Whatever your 10 is, it is waaay down at one end of that ruler.

Your **ugly 10** *absolutely is* a reason to have stress. Your ugly 10 is valid. Your ugly 10 is awful…and you felt it down to your core.

On that ruler, notice you have the following numbers remaining:

~ 9, 8, 7, 6, 5, 4, 3, 2, 1~

You know what your 10 looks like.

When things come at you in life, when you start feeling stressed (pounding heart, can't breathe, feeling angry…), put a number on the 1-10 scale and compare it to your ugly 10.

PUT A NUMBER ON IT!

Is what's happening now as bad as your ugly TEN? Is it as bad as when your parents got divorced or you lost a loved one?

What number would you put on what's bothering you right now? The issue might be a 1 or 2. Maybe it's even a 5 or higher, but it's probably not a 10.

Think of your 10.

Now, think about what is stressing you at this moment in time. Put a number on it (remember to compare it to your 10).

Problems happen all day long. Treating every one of them like a 10 actually puts stress on your body. That stress causes the body to begin to age very quickly. If you are at a 10 all day long, your heart will get tired, and you will be mentally exhausted. This is when good tenacity skills can step in and help.

When you start noticing your heart beating faster, your stomach clenching and feel that stress rage coming, put a number on what's happening.

Ask yourself, "Is this a 10?"

If not, don't treat it like it's a 10.

3

THIRD, CHALLENGE THOSE
"WEIRD THOUGHTS" WHEN THEY POP UP.

When you find yourself thinking your friends hate you, ask yourself, "Then, why are they my friends?" When you think you'll never make it to college, create a list of some college graduates who were unlikely to make it but are huge successes now. Every single negative thought you have can be challenged.

How you look at things changes the way you think about them. If you didn't finish your homework *again*, instead of saying, "Oh well, my teacher hates me anyway. I'm a loser and can't do anything right," try saying, "Time management is a skill, not a talent! I can ask for help to learn this skill. I can go in for tutoring. I'll get to school early and finish it."

4

FOURTH, BEWARE OF THE LITTLE GRAY SNAKE.

Early in my career, I worked with a stress management clinic. I had one man in the group who was particularly stressed, almost to the point where he was shaking. He was so uptight, I thought he was going to explode.

I told him, "I think you need a vacation, sir."

He followed my advice and took a trip to the beach. As he was walking along the cliffs overlooking the vast blue ocean and watching the sunset, he looked down at his path. All of a sudden there was a snake! A slithering gray snake!!

Now, most people are afraid of snakes. Snakes give them quite the panic attack and stress reaction! That gentleman came back to the stress management clinic the following week and told everyone about how the snake came right for him. He was mad at me because I told him to go relax at the beach and there was a snake out there!

"Was it one of those little gray snakes?" I asked.

"Yes!"

I smiled. "Sir, you don't have to worry about those little gray snakes. They are not poisonous! That snake was not going to kill you."

He glared back at me. "If that little gray snake chases me over the edge of the cliff, and I drop forty feet to my death, it didn't HAVE to be poisonous to kill me. It just chased me over the edge!!!"

How many little gray snakes do you have in your day that are chasing you over the edge?

Go back to your ruler, your scale of 1 to 10. Are there a lot of 1-5 situations that you are treating like 10s? Do you have a lot of little things going on in your life that aren't causing much stress but still feel like 10s? What little gray snake issues do you have that you are blowing way out of proportion? Are you allowing those little gray snake issues to take you over the edge?

Put a number on these little problems. Don't treat them all like 10s. Don't allow them to chase you over the edge.

STRESS MANAGEMENT 101 RECAP

Those four steps again:

1. Ask yourself: "Can I control this situation?"
2. Change the way you look at what is bothering you.
3. Challenge those "weird thoughts" when they pop up.
4. Beware of the little gray snake.

Remember, when you start feeling those signs and symptoms that tell you that you're getting stressed, when you feel like you are going from a 1 to a 5 on that stress scale…use these four steps to bring yourself back down, so you can handle the challenges you are facing.

FINDING THE ENERGY TO BALANCE LIFE

Life is hard and there are days when everyone wants a piece of you. Chores to do, siblings to help, demands from friends, homework, ugh!! How do you find the energy to do all this?

There are 4 Ps that can help you with tenacity and finding balance in your life, the healthy way:

1. Proper Exercise
2. Proper Eating
3. Proper Rest
4. Proper Attitude

Proper Exercise. Exercising every day is a great way to burn off some anxiety. Being involved in sports at school works for some, but for others, just putting on your favorite music and going for a walk in the neighborhood works.

Do you have a dog? Does the dog need to walk? Even dogs get lazy and become overweight. Take that dog for a walk every day. It will do you both some good. This is a healthy coping skill to take into adulthood.

Proper Eating. Are you eating to live or living to eat? What do your eating habits look like? If you often feel moody, tired or unmotivated, it could be because of what you're eating. When you have good eating habits with plenty of protein, fruits and veggies, it helps balance you from the inside out and can help control how moody or quick to anger you feel. I'm not saying don't ever grab that candy bar, just eat a yogurt or some other protein with it. Protein can help balance the sugar you put in your body.

Proper Rest. I often hear people say that teenagers sleep a lot. Is that true? Do they need it? They do, but most are not getting enough. And it's not just teens who are tired. I've read that 60% of adults don't get enough sleep either. If you are taking your problems to bed and juggling them all night or taking your phone to bed, you won't get good, quality sleep. You will be tired and moody the next day. Here are my top three ways to get better rest:

- ✓ Try putting your phone away at least thirty minutes before going to sleep. The light coming off the phone can cause you to have a bad night's sleep. Even if you have it on dark (or night) mode.

- ✓ Try giving yourself a break. Are you going to bed and doing the *I should have… I could have… I would have…* all night? Instead, think of all the things that went well that day.

- ✓ Try positivity. Are you overthinking all your problems and finding it hard to sleep? Get comfortable in bed and imagine your goals. What would your life look like if you accomplished those goals? Imagine it so hard that you actually feel in control, feel good, feel safe. Allow yourself to drift off to sleep in this calm state.

Proper Attitude. How would you describe your attitude in life, overall? How do you feel about life? Are you happy all the time? Nothing gets you down? You hear the birds chirping, and you sing along? Do you always see the bright side of life? You may be an optimist. Or do you run on the side of being dark and moody? Life sucks and is never fun. You may be more of a pessimist. Which describes your attitude? Maybe you are somewhere in the middle.

How can you shift to having more of an optimistic attitude? Research tells us that optimistic people are happier and tend to live longer than pessimists. One reason for their optimism is that they can put a number on things that come at them in life. They don't get weighed down by treating everything like it's a 10…like it's the end of the world.

These 4 Ps (Proper Exercise, Proper Eating, Proper Rest, and a Proper Attitude) are the strongest tools you can use to maintain tenacity. No, they cannot make every problem disappear. By using your tenacity and reaching out to your counselor, teacher or other trusted person in your life, you can learn to manage what comes at you every day.

You have a team of people who love and care about you. They want to help.

HOMEWORK:

1. How do you handle it when you start feeling stress?

2. What is your ugly TEN on your stress scale?

3. What are the little gray snakes in your life that take you over the edge (things you are treating like a 10 but are really only a 1 or a 2)?

SELF-REFLECTION:

The goal of tenacity is learning how to recognize what you are feeling, putting a number on it, and reacting to it in a healthy way. This is easier to do when you exercise, eat well, get proper rest and have a good attitude in life. You picked out your clothes this morning. Did you pick out a good attitude?

TIPS FOR TEACHERS:

Sometimes the kids who need the most love are the ones who are the hardest to love, like Samir. Often, those with anger, frustration, and serious rage issues are the most scared and alone. They need someone to be their champion.

It is too easy to give up on them. It is too easy to not like them or to give anger and attitude right back to them.

These are the kids who don't like anyone. Most of the time, they don't even like themselves. They hate the world and everyone in it. These are the kids who, once you win them over, are your kids for life.

How do we reach kids like this?

By not giving up. Everyone has already given up on them. To an extent, they have given up on themselves. For all of their posturing and angry demeanor, their confidence is in the gutter.

Mrs. Rose understood this. As angry as she was at Samir's behavior, she still cared enough to reach out to people who she knew could help her student. She knew he cared about football, so she had the football coach talk with him. She hoped this would help to motivate him with his homework and classwork while still allowing him to continue playing football. She also reached out to his counselor who could give Samir referrals and resources to help him work on his anger and soft skills.

The teacher never has to put up with disrespectful behavior, and there will be consequences for Samir's negative actions. But most important, the teacher can commit to starting each new day fresh, to control her frustrations and anger towards the student. The teacher can also keep the counselor, coach, and parent updated on her student's academic, social, and mental health progress.

Hopefully, our students will eventually see us teachers as their allies rather than their adversaries. By never giving up on them, even when it would be VERY easy to, we build trust and open the door for having a positive relationship whenever our students are ready.

COUNSELOR'S THOUGHTS:

Samir feels anger...*rage*. He says that he always feels that way because of others, like his mom and Mrs. Rose. He says their constant nagging makes him angry, but it really stems from a lack of healthy coping skills.

Samir has gone through an incredible amount of personal family trauma. He has never addressed any of the feelings or deep emotions that come with his heavy burden of life experiences.

Unchecked, his emotions of abandonment, sadness, anger, resentment, and family responsibility have turned this young man into a raw nerve of rage.

I would make a recommendation for a counselor referral with an outside agency that partners with the school to work with Samir on healthy coping strategies. I would also make a standing weekly, one-on-one session for Samir. This would allow me to review his grades, see how his family life is going, and gauge his resilience.

Because Samir struggles with time management, together we could look over his class schedule to see if a study hall can be worked into his day. This would help him stay on top of his classwork. I could also give him resources for developing his time management skills at home. This would help stop him constantly blaming others for his lateness, missing assignments, and ducking responsibilities.

Samir's tardiness is mostly a result of him staying up too late because he was on his phone "escaping."

Many teens (and adults) often scroll through their phones when they are feeling stressed, overwhelmed, or bored. The habit of scrolling serves mainly as an escape from the issues at hand and our responsibilities.

I would encourage Samir to use the alarm feature on his phone to set up time limits to help reduce the amount of time he spends scrolling through social media and enable him to spend time on other activities. Like homework.

In fact, students like Samir would benefit from a daily schedule.

For example, study hall could be from 3:00-4:00; practice from 4:00-6:00; dinner from 6:30-7:00; homework from 7:00-8:30; 8:30-9:30 is phone time. The phone would lock after 9:30, allowing him a good night's rest.

Teachers, counselors, and principals all want to see our students succeed. One factor for student success is attendance. If counselors see a student is late to class *consistently* (9 out of 10 times), there is more to their story. A counselor's job is to listen to their story, their life, their REASON...and really SEE the student.

Students often think teachers and parents want to make their lives miserable because they continue to nag them about all the work that still needs to be done. They nag them about practice, their friends, their homework.

As a counselor, I often hear, "They don't care about me! They betrayed me!"

This couldn't be further from the truth.

It's good to remind our students that if their parents and teachers honestly didn't care, they would be completely okay with letting them fail their classes. They wouldn't care if the student didn't graduate. They wouldn't care if they got kicked off the team. Samir's mom, Mrs. Rose, and his coach are trying to help him in the form of reminders, holding him accountable for his actions, and referring him to the counselor.

At the same time, it can really help to *show* Samir how much he is cared for. To improve the relationship between teachers and their students, I would encourage them to get more involved.

For example, Mrs. Rose could attend one of Samir's games.

Having his teacher cheer him on and demonstrate an interest in his life outside of the classroom would help them connect better. When teachers make that extra effort to invest in their students' interests, students find themselves investing more effort in their classes.

As the counselor, I would reach out to his parent. Parental involvement is key to helping Samir work out some of the issues that he is experiencing at home.

Together with his therapist, Samir's mom could help him work through his feelings and frustrations.

SAMIR'S OUTCOME:

Samir was blaming everyone else for his problems. When he felt anger coming on, he was quick to act on it. He knew he had to make a change, or he'd risk losing football.

The meeting with the counselor led to Samir being referred to a low-cost therapist. There, Samir was able to voice his feelings and frustrations. He had a healthy outlet.

The therapist helped him see that he, his teachers, his counselor, and his coach were all on the same team.

They ALL cared about him.

The therapist worked with him on how to handle conflict and how to cope when he had big feelings.

Samir's grades eventually got better because he improved his ability to control his anger and his time management skills. With better grades, he was able to play football all four years of high school.

Samir went on to play football for a local community college.

Chapter 3

DEIDRE'S STORY

"*La familia lo es todo!*" *my parents say to me. Every. Single. Day. In English, it means, "Family is everything." To my parents, it means my loyalty must always be with my family. To me, it means that I was born to take care of them, forever.*

My parents are an older couple who struggled to have children. When they finally had me, they were in their forties, and I became everything to them. I am an only child, so everything gets dumped on me. I'm not talking about doing all the housework, but about caring for them as they age and fulfilling their hopes and dreams and expectations for my life.

As a child of immigrant parents, they remind me over and over about the sacrifices they made for "la familia." They came here from Mexico, escaping poverty and neighborhood drug lords to give me the best life possible. They have spent their time, effort and money to give me this modest but clean home, to put food on the table, to have enough money for clothes and necessities.

In return, I'm expected to be the perfect daughter who lives up to her parent's dreams and wishes. They expect me to get married right after high school and bring their grandchildren into the world. That is all they have ever wanted and expected of me.

But what about my *dreams?*

Do I just bury my goals and live the life they want, or do I dare to dream? The guilt over this is a huge weight on my shoulders. Especially now.

I don't want to be a stay-at-home wife and mother. I want more. I want to go away to college. I don't want to be their perfect Mexican-American daughter, living only to have babies, and I know once they hear this, it will nearly kill them.

I was always a bad student. Growing up, I couldn't even read until the 3rd grade. Turns out, I was tested at school and have a severe case of dyslexia.

With dyslexia, the words and letters and symbols get mixed up in my head. It is a learning disability I've always struggled with. I got help from school and my teachers, but because I was already so behind everyone else, I figured, "Why try? I'll never catch up."

To be honest, I didn't put in my full effort.

No, let's be COMPLETELY honest: I put in zero effort.

I failed everything, and my parents' disappointment hurt. They were my parents. If they didn't believe in me, why should I believe in myself?

Elementary and middle school were easy; I did nothing, and they passed me anyway. Cool beans! Why would high school be any different?

I got to high school and fell in with a crowd who thought the same way I did. We all thought school was just about having a good time. School sucks. After all, we were just expected to become wives and mothers anyway. You don't need geometry to cook and clean a house. You don't need to know how to write an essay to care for children. School didn't matter. We just had to put in the time until we could get out and become what our parents wanted us to become.

Then came junior year…

Within weeks, my high school counselor, Ms. Hall, called me into her office. She let me know that I was not going to graduate with my current grades.

I laughed in her face and smirked. "Ms. Hall, you and I both KNOW they are going to keep passing me along, and I'll graduate." Her threats didn't scare me. Still smiling smugly, I told her, "They've tried to do this all my life. Grades never mattered. I always passed regardless of my grades. I'm not stupid. I'm nobody's fool."

Ms. Hall said, "I thought you might say that, so I brought in a senior, Esteban, to tell you about his journey. Then, maybe you can see what I'm trying to get through to you."

At that moment, a boy, almost a man, came in and said hello to me. I said, "Hi,"
awkwardly, wondering what the heck was going on.

"Like you," Esteban said, "I was failing everything. I thought the same things
you did. That they were just going to pass all students." He laughed softly. "I was
a fool. Last year, I was a junior. Most of my friends were seniors, and we would all
ditch classes together and walk around the school. Our teachers were glad we weren't
in their classes ruining all their lessons with our antics. We thought we were badass.
Turns out, we were the dummies.

"NONE of my senior friends graduated last year. They couldn't believe it. Their
parents got parties ready for them, but the day of graduation came and went. They
didn't get to walk across that stage. They never got diplomas. They got nothing. And
now, they have no jobs on top of that. They can't even get a basic McDonald's job
without high school diplomas. Their parents are so disappointed in them and kicked
them out. Now, they couch surf at anyone's house who will let them. No girls want to
date them, and they have no place to stay and no food to eat."

My mouth was agape. "You're kidding! There's no way they wouldn't pass us!"

Esteban shrugged. "Hey, if you want to be as dumb as them, then go for it. Just
know, you had a full warning. You don't have to believe me. Trust me, I actually
would rather be in class right now. If I don't pass English this year, I won't graduate
either."

"So, you might still pass? I thought you said you failed everything?"

"I did. But then I took summer school and credit recovery to make up the classes. Turns out, I'm pretty smart. My counselor," he looked at Ms. Hall, *"looked at my test scores and saw that I had potential. She signed me up for every make-up class I could fit into my current schedule and credit recovery after school. I spent the entire summer in summer school. My new grades are the ones that will count on my transcript for college. It's like the Fs were never there."* He beamed with pride. *"It's not easy. It was freaking HARD. But I knew I wanted to be something in this life and college is my way to advance myself and my family's lives."*

College, *I thought.* I wonder what college would be like. *But then I stopped myself. I live in reality.*

Ms. Hall, the counselor, locked eyes with me. "You, Deidre, are in a very similar boat. Your grades are not good. However, your state test scores are not bad. They are even, dare I say, on the good side. You can be more than just a truant student who does nothing with her life. You can **be** *anything. You can* **do** *anything. Your life is bigger than you think. I believe in YOU. Do YOU believe in you?"*

I sat there in shock.

NO ONE had EVER told me that I could do ANYthing.

I thought I would just be cooking and cleaning for the rest of my life. That's when I realized that if things didn't change, I would have nothing to look forward to.

I did NOT want to cook, clean, and wipe baby butts my whole adult life.

I wanted to go away to college. I wanted to be something bigger than I thought was possible. Could I dare imagine this life? If yes, what would be the next steps?

I left the counselor's office after signing up for credit recovery in summer school. I also signed up for weekend classes at the local community college that would count for high school and college credit.

I had a dream, and I wanted to make it a reality.

I started showing up to my classes and was shocked at how far behind I was. I started going to tutoring every day at lunch. Slowly but surely, my grades came up. My hard work changed all the Fs in my previous classes to As.

I checked in with Ms. Hall once a week. She helped me with coping skills, time management and even reached out to my teachers a few times when I needed help on assignments. This continued until October of my senior year.

It was finally time to submit college applications. I wanted to go far away. I wanted to go to Los Angeles or New York. I wanted to live the big city life and get out of this little town. I wanted to feel the rush and thrill of city life.

When it came time to choose a major, Ms. Hall looked at me and said, "Well, what do you want to be? You can do anything."

When she said those words to me, I believed her with my whole heart. She had been with me this entire time, holding my hand.

She was my lifeline, my safe adult. Most of all: She SAW me. She really SAW me. She KNEW I was capable of much more than I knew.

"I want to be a school counselor," I told her, "just like you. I want kids to feel like they have options. That they can be anything they want to be. A lot of kids don't have that kind of positivity and love in their life. I want to make a difference like you've made a difference in my life. My life has been changed because of you."

Her eyes filled with tears. "I KNOW you will positively impact every person who comes in contact with you. You make the world a better place, just by being in it. Thank you so much for seeing what I already saw: your potential."

We hit "submit," and my application was officially on its way. What a joyous moment! But I knew in the back of my mind, it was going to be a horrible time at home. This news was going to kill my aging, weak parents. I prayed this news wouldn't give them a heart attack.

When I got my acceptance letter to New York University, I opened it with Ms. Hall. It included a full scholarship. We sobbed together with joy!

Now it is real. All that hard work has paid off. But…

Now, I have to break the news to my parents.

I go home. My parents are in the kitchen. I ask them to sit down and put the acceptance letter on the table in front of them. I tell them to read it.

After they read it, they slowly look at me with wide eyes.

My father says, "Why do you want to leave your family? After EVERYTHING we have done for you! We saved you from poverty in Mexico and came to America to give YOU a better life. We put a roof over your head and fed you food made with our own hands! We've given you the BEST life possible. You are our ONE and ONLY child. And now you are going to…" he bursts into tears, "to LEAVE us! You DON'T do that! **La familia lo es todo!**" he shouts.

He holds my mom, and they both sob tears of sadness and despair into each other. They look like I have died. And perhaps I have. Their expectations of me have died on this very day. My heart sinks. But I think of how hard I have worked to get to this point. I took credit recovery until 7 p.m. every night. I stayed up until 2 a.m. doing homework. I spent my whole summer and weekends making up classes.

I have sacrificed my sleep, time with friends and family and my sanity to achieve this goal. But as I look into their eyes filled with disappointment…that guilt—that family guilt—stabs me in the gut.

It hurts me to see them so sad. How can I possibly leave them? How can I be so selfish?

After all, "La familia lo es todo…"

TENACITY

The ability to not give up.

The ability to keep going

even when you don't want to or

even when you don't think you can.

Have you ever been so overwhelmed with homework assignments, Mom's never-ending list for you to do, friends and their drama, and you feel like you can't deal with it? Do you hear yourself saying, "I don't need this! I'm so sick of this! I'm done! I don't care anymore!"

That is what tenacity is not.

Tenacity is about recognizing when you are getting overwhelmed and trying some of those stress management techniques from the last chapter. Notice the signs your body is giving you (the racing heart, it's hard to breathe, feeling like you are going to explode). Rate your stress level.

What number is it on that scale of 1-5? Take a few deep breaths. Take the dog out for a quick walk.

Tenacity is regrouping and bringing your body back down to a balanced point, both mentally and physically. It's about getting your head around what's overwhelming you and getting your body relaxed so you can think clearly.

Tenacity is taking one step forward and moving towards your goals. It is making a plan and breaking down what's being asked of you so that it feels more like bite-sized pieces. Tenacity is reading and re-reading your goals every day, even when you get overwhelmed.

Tenacity is staying focused and staying strong.

WHEN DOES TENACITY START?

Developing tenacity doesn't happen all in one day. It takes time to build, practice and strengthen. Luckily for freshmen, this is the one year when the greatest expectation of you is to get used to this phase of your education. Then your sophomore, junior and senior years each require a certain amount of tenacity and focus.

Sophomore year of high school. Sophomore tenacity is about starting the year off strong! During your freshman year, you were getting to know the school and learning what's expected of you.

By sophomore year, you should know what's expected of you—from the beginning.

The biggest issue a sophomore has is time management.

The two most common phrases sophomores say about their homework is, "I'll do it later. I have a lot of time."

They say, "I have a book report on *Great Expectations* due at the end of the month. I'll start reading it the night before it's due."

That just isn't going to happen. It's about 550 pages.

Are you the one who comes up with the many excuses when your teacher asks, "Why didn't you get your homework done and turned in?"

- ✓ My sister spilled peanut butter on it, then it fell on the floor, and the dog ate it.
- ✓ I had it done and in my backpack, but my dog peed on my backpack.
- ✓ I was doing my homework, but the VMAs came on, and my friend and I were on the phone watching it together. I thought the VMAs were over at 9:00, but they went until 11:00…and that's why I didn't get my homework done.

Tenacity and time management means taking accountability for knowing what is due and taking the responsibility to get it done by managing your time well. It means figuring how long it will take for you to read that book and putting in the time to get it done.

For example, here's how you can manage your time expectations, with a 550-page book like *Great Expectations*, so you can finish on time:

1. Set the timer on your phone for one hour. Read as many pages as you can in that one hour. How many did you read? Let's say you got through 28 pages in an hour…not too bad!

2. How many hours will it take to read the whole book? If the book is 550 pages, and you read 28 pages in one hour, it's going to take you just about **20 hours** to finish that book. *Do the math: Divide the total pages by how many pages you read in that 1 hour (550 total pages / 28 pages read in 1 hour = 19.6 = 20 total hours).*

3. This means you'll need to read for one hour a day, 5 days a week, to finish that book in a month. Be realistic. Don't leave it until the night before. *Do the math: Divide the total hours needed to read the book by how many weeks you have, then divide that by five weekdays (20 hours / 4 weeks = 5 hours per week; 5 hours per week / 5 weekdays per week = 1 hour per weekday).*

Tenacity and time management means being realistic about the amount of time it will take to get homework done.

Junior year of high school. This is a BIG year for tenacity. Grades matter this year, so look at your GPA. Ask, "Do I need to work extra hard this year to get my GPA up to at least a 3.0? Can I take credit recovery? If your SAT/ACTs are lower than you need, take the tests again throughout the year. This shows tenacity!

You may have something called "test anxiety." This is where you study and prepare, but when it comes to the day of the test, you sit down, and your brain freezes.

All that information you studied: gone.

Just the thought of taking the test brings on the fast heartbeat, the head pounding, the stomach clenching, the fear, the anxiety, and you can't breathe.

Test anxiety and brain freeze-up happen to a lot of teens—adults too! Some of the stress management techniques you just learned in the last chapter can help when this happens.

Practice this. When you sit down to take a test:

1. Take some deep breaths.
2. Count slowly to 5, breathing in as you count. Breathe out to a count of 5. Repeat.

3. If you read the first test question and still have a "frozen brain," circle it and move on to the next question. Get to a question where you know the answer and feel the information starting to flow out of the brain. Now you are golden. Go back and answer all the circled questions because your brain is now unfrozen.

Have tenacity! Learn and practice the above exercise to relax your brain before a test, and the information will flow. The more you practice this at test-taking time, the easier it will get.

VOLUNTEERING

Junior year also means reaching out and getting involved in volunteer work. Volunteer on Saturdays at your local library, a museum in town, church, the local food bank, the YMCA, Boys & Girls Clubs or animal shelters. You can also join a club at school that does volunteer work if you don't want to give up your Saturdays. Look into the Interact Club or Best Buddies.

These volunteer hours are not paid, but they show tenacity. Volunteering shows you are a well-rounded person who cares about others; you are not just the sum of your GPA. You've got what it takes to achieve your goals.

Volunteering is a fantastic way to develop your character. It can help you find out who you are. It can also show you what you like and don't like in people, all the while practicing your tenacity.

I was a "tough" mom. I required all four of my kids to earn 1,000 hours of volunteer work throughout their high school years. That comes down to 250 hours of volunteering each year. I knew their grades were not top of the class. This commitment to volunteering and giving back to the community would help balance that out.

Remember, you are more than the sum of your GPA.

When my boys volunteered at the local YMCA, they were basketball coaches for the 6–12 age group. They were scared at first because they didn't think they were all that great at basketball, but I told them, "You are better than a 6-year-old, so to them, you are like Kobe." They had one practice a week and one game on Saturday. They coached with their friends, making the experience more fun for all of them.

Volunteering also let them practice talking to the kids' parents, which can be scary. They learned how to get comfortable communicating with adults about their children. Working with kids and adults are good skills to practice and take into adulthood, especially for someone planning to work with children in their future.

All this volunteering paid off.

When they went on to apply to college with their 2.7 or 3.0 GPAs, it was those 1,000 hours of volunteering that got them accepted. Those 1,000 hours showed the college, "I am dedicated. I am motivated. I take pride in what I do. I have tenacity."

NOT JUST RECORDING YOUR HOURS...

Get a folder and label it, "Tenacity." When you start volunteering, use this folder to keep track of all the hours you spend volunteering.

But don't stop there. Ask for a letter of recommendation from each organization when your volunteer time is over! Put your letters in your folder. After each volunteer session, my kids asked for and received letters of recommendation, which they used during the application process. They knew what many students unfortunately do not know:

Including letters of recommendation along with volunteer hours when applying to colleges could put you ahead of other applicants.

Yes, the hours are important, but how do you think colleges will respond to the high praises of well-respected leaders?

For our family, the response to all four of my kids was: ACCEPTED! They all went on to college.

Volunteer Checklist:

✓ Sign up to volunteer.

✓ Keep track of your hours.

✓ Do a good job!

✓ Get written letters of recommendation from each organization (keep your hours and letters in your tenacity folder).

✓ Include the hours and letters of recommendation in your college applications packets.

Senior year of high school. By senior year you should have tenacity down, be applying to colleges or trade schools, and finishing the year strong.

Recently, a Supreme Court decision ended affirmative action for college admissions. Colleges no longer give an advantage to minority students. They evaluate your application the same as they do all the applications of the other kids applying. This includes those kids who had help and every advantage given to them.

Show them how well-rounded you are, not just your GPA.

Show them where you came from, your struggles, your family's struggles and how through tenacity, you never let go of your dreams.

You volunteered, committed to a sport, helped raised your siblings. Now you are applying today, asking for a chance to go to their college or trade school.

What makes you different, what makes you stand out?

Maybe your parents don't speak English, and you have had to translate for them everywhere. You have worked since you were fourteen and have given the money to your family for food.

You didn't give up.

You have tenacity.

In your application, colleges want to see the entire person who is applying. Your challenges actually make you a good candidate for their college, trade school…or for any job!

In your senior year, work on keeping those grades up. Finish the year strong; it shows tenacity from start to finish. Many colleges and trade schools require you to send them your final semester grades to see if you actually had the tenacity to finish strong and not give up at the end.

WHAT KILLS TENACITY?

What kills the drive, the goals, the dream? Ask your parents what they wanted to be after they got out of high school. Ask, "Where did you see yourself going when you were graduating high school? What did you want to do in your life? Did it happen? Why not? What killed that dream?"

You may hear stories about how *their* parents told them they weren't smart enough. They may have been told, "Our culture doesn't go to college." Maybe they were guilt-tripped into staying home to take care of their parents…because that's what family does.

I always think about the movie, *My Big Fat Greek Wedding* when the dad says, "Why do you want to leave me?"

Family guilt can feel overwhelming.

What else kills the drive, the goals, the dream?

It's ANGER, BITTERNESS and REGRET.

And yes. Maybe you have good reason to feel this way. I am not dismissing what you may have gone through or are going through now.

But you have a choice. Will you overcome through tenacity and choose what you want your life to be? Or will you let your experiences choose your life for you because you're hurt or angry?

Being angry is like somebody putting a steaming, hot coal in YOUR hand, and telling you to hold it tightly and hope your enemy gets burned. Here you are, holding this hot, burning coal in your hand and hoping everyone who's ever done you wrong gets burned.

Doesn't make much sense, does it?

You've got to decide to let the anger and those grudges go. That anger is like a big, dark cloud over your head that everyone sees. Everyone can tell you are angry. Is that what you want to be known for? Being the angry kid over there?

Or are you one of those teens who blames everyone else for things that have gone wrong in their life? Tenacity means taking accountability for you, and only you. It's not the dog's fault, or the VMAs fault that they were on until 11 p.m.

Some teens are angry because they feel they got a bad deal in life. They landed in a "less than perfect" family that hates them. Their life sucks. Well, guess what? Everyone lands in that less-than-perfect family and has issues to overcome, not just you. Even those who seem to live a charmed life have issues no one knows about.

I see teens who are so bitter and angry about what happened in kindergarten, and they can't let that go. Some are still carrying this around ten years later. People change, they grow up and mature. Who or what is making you bitter and angry? Use your tenacity to rise above that bitterness.

Then there's the "jerk factor."

If you ever find yourself thinking your mom is a jerk, your dad is a jerk, your teacher is a jerk, your friends are being jerks, your brother's a jerk…

Go look in the mirror because the jerk may just be… <u>YOU</u>.

People react to you and how you come across. If you smile at someone, chances are they will smile back. If you are giving dirty looks, whether on purpose or not, everyone will see your dark cloud and react by being a jerk back to you.

All these possible versions of you can be overcome. It all boils down to: Do you have tenacity?

DO I HAVE TENACITY?

Tenacity is: "How bad do I want it?"

If my goal is to become a nurse, I'm probably going to have to go to college. If I want to be an auto mechanic, I'm going to have to go to trade school or community college.

Whatever your goal is in life, write it on a piece of paper and tape it to your bed. Tape it to the bathroom mirror, tape it to your nightstand. Look at it EVERY morning, after school and before bed.

Keep that goal in mind, even when you are saying, "To heck with this… I'm done… This isn't worth it."

Stay focused. Stay strong.

Tenacity isn't about having a lot of money or how smart you are.

A lot of teens say, "I'll never go to college because I'm not that smart." Not everyone needs to be that smart to go to college. They just need to have tenacity.

Remember, all four of my kids went to college. Did each one have a 4.99 GPA? One did, but the other three struggled with dyslexia, ADD, OCD and other learning disabilities. Every single day was a struggle with reading and homework. My kids learned there are things they had to do to get where they wanted to be in life. If you want to achieve your goals, you have to practice that tenacity.

Tenacity is believing in YOU! Your goals. Your dreams. It's proving to a college, a trade school, a future employer that you are a well-rounded person. You aren't just the sum of your GPA.

You are more than that.

WHAT ARE YOUR GOALS?

If your dream career involves going to college or a trade school, the requirements are pretty spelled out for you. Colleges require high school students to complete A through G classes. Trade schools have their requirements, too. Your school counselor can help you put these courses into your schedule.

If you are not sure what your goals are, ask your counselor about taking an interest inventory survey. This short quiz will help you set a goal based on your interests. Remember, when you have a career doing something you love, it will never feel like work.

What are colleges and trade schools looking for in you? What do employers look for when you come in and apply for a job? They are looking for TENACITY.

Colleges and trade schools look to see if you started each school year strong, *and* did you finish strong? Did you have tenacity throughout the year, or did you fizzle out and give up? Did you get Bs and Cs the first semester, and then your report card showed Ds and Fs after the second semester? This says volumes about you…you gave up, and that is not having tenacity.

Did you skip volunteering in your freshman year but started up in your sophomore year and even added hours in your junior and senior years? Did you join a sport and stick with it even when it was hard or when you weren't the star player? This also says volumes about you... you worked harder, and that is having tenacity.

You are a combination of your grades, your volunteer work, your community service, sports involvement, etc. They are looking to see if you have the tenacity to balance all these things, in order to achieve your goals.

TAKE ACCOUNTABILITY

No one is perfect. We all make mistakes along the way. It's what you DO with those mistakes to make it right. It's not about blaming the dog, the teacher or your mom.

Even if you stumbled along the way and had a bad semester, did you take accountability for it?

Did you go to credit recovery?

Did you take the class over in summer school?

That shows tenacity.

One of my kids was a gifted athlete and played high school basketball. The bus left school at 6th period to travel to away games. His schedule had him in Algebra during 6th period, so he missed a lot of lessons and flunked the class.

He still made it into college because he took the class over in summer school and passed.

That shows tenacity.

HOMEWORK:

1. What goals did your parents have in high school?

2. What killed their dreams? What regrets do they have?

3. What are your goals? How bad do you want them?

SELF-REFLECTION:

Tenacity. How bad do you want it? Look at your goals from #3 above and write them down on a separate paper. Tape the paper to the night-stand, the bathroom mirror, the bed. Read your goals every morning, afternoon and night. Read your goals especially when you hear yourself saying, "This isn't worth it." It *IS* worth it.

Did you write your goals down above? Do it now.

TIPS FOR TEACHERS:

As teachers, we come across so many students like Deidre. Students who want a better life. Students who want to advance through education. But many of these students are navigating family cultures and parental expectations.

Familial guilt can be a barrier to them accomplishing their goals. Most of the time, it stops them from even trying in school. Having someone who believes in students like Deidre (as her school counselor did) makes all the difference in those students' lives, even when they can't see it themselves.

Sometimes our students come to us with very little academic success. Most don't get enough encouragement at home. Watch for those who need your support. When students are making an effort and trying, it's important to let them know that we see them. Give them positive reinforcement because that is a powerful motivator. We see their potential even when no one else does. Our encouragement helps students see they have options, and from there…the sky is the limit!

Also, it can be very helpful to have older students like Esteban come into your classes and talk to students about what can happen if they follow a negative path. Students may not believe adults, especially when some adults have lied to them in their past. But if an older student shares their perspective, it can make it more real to the students. It can open their eyes to what the future may hold, both positive and negative.

I recommend that teachers create a way to communicate with parents. Educate them on the benefits of allowing their children to move forward and even move away. Some parents want their children to go to the local community college or start working right away. They need food on the table now, not in four years or whenever their children will finish college. It is hard to delay that gratification when your family is hungry.

Parents need their older children to stay home and take care of the younger siblings so that they can work and keep a roof over their heads. Many are afraid their children will leave and never come back or visit.

Teachers can show parents that by holding their children hostage, the children may end up resenting their family for forcing them to stay home. Some children may leave and never come back just because of that resentment.

As a young adult, our students need to make adult choices, for better or worse. They need the parent to be the wind beneath their wings and allow them to fly. As teachers, we can facilitate this conversation and perhaps make a difference for many students who would otherwise get lost in this cycle.

COUNSELOR'S THOUGHTS:

This story demonstrates how school counselors can motivate their students. Ms. Hall supported Deidre over her high school years. She checked in with her often. Ms. Hall showed her that she was in her corner. She helped Deidre find her goals, plan her next steps and see a future—even when Deidre didn't believe in herself.

Always remember that a counselor has a powerful voice, and when used in combination with the teacher, we can transition our teens into seeing themselves as successful adults in the future.

PASSING THE BATON.

As counselors, we must also fully understand the very real area of concern in this chapter. The biggest hurdle for many students like Deidre is the push-and-pull dynamics they feel when they realize their own personal goals, dreams and aspirations are not in line with what others think.

The future a teen envisions may look quite different from what their parents wanted for them or different from what their culture expects of them.

Parents often think of their children as a continuation of themselves: "copy, paste, and repeat."

Only, generations are no longer in a copy, paste, and repeat situation. Students today should not be expected to do the exact same thing as their parents did. They have unique experiences, newer technologies, and goals that can take them past the limitations their parents had.

It's important to let our students know they can remain a strong part of their family and culture while still taking advantage of the opportunity to go beyond, dream big and find a future they want.

Parents run their "leg" of the relay race, only to pass the baton off to their children as they begin their journey and path in life.

The challenge is that many parents don't actually ever let the baton go. They often want their children to stay close, to care for them in their old age and never leave them. They want their children to value and believe in what they believe in.

Most parents don't know the job of passing the baton is not to clip their children's wings. The job is to impart the wisdom, values and experiences that made parents successful down to their children. Then watch the children soar.

Parents have had their turn!

They ran their 'leg' of the race; it is now the student's turn.

Our students' paths may be the same or different than that of their parents, but it's ultimately up to the student. Once the baton is passed, a parent's job is to cheer their child on as they watch and support them running their leg of the race.

Our job as counselors is to work with and help support our students in finding their passion and their dreams. We help them reflect on their identity and their place in the world. We help them find their strengths and set realistic goals to help them achieve what they've only dared to dream.

As Deidre faces the guilt and cultural stereotypes her parents have placed on her, it's important for the counselor to get her partnered with the school's mental health agency, so she has support.

As she ventures into her leg of the race, she will be forever trying to balance these cultural expectations and family obligations.

Having that mental support will help her foster her newfound self-confidence and tenacity as she achieves her goals. With technology,

Deidre will always be able to stay close to her parents and ultimately, to care for them in their old age.

DEIDRE'S OUTCOME:

Deidre didn't even realize she wanted to go to college until her junior year. When she told her parents, they felt betrayed, and she knew she couldn't leave them.

But then, tenacity gave her the strength to straighten her shoulders and rewrite her future.

Tenacity gave her the courage to tell them that she had received a scholarship and was choosing to go to college.

Tenacity gave her the grit to say, "I love you both very much. You gave me the world. And now I'm going to give it back to you."

Deidre had the tenacity to sit through the difficult conversation with her confused parents. She knew everything they did was to give her a better life, and now going to college was the way for her to live that better life.

With a college degree, she could earn more money. With a good job, she could help out the family, give them (and her future family) a better life.

She knew that pursuing her goal was because "La familia lo es todo."

She told them, "This will make me happy."

Her parents accepted her choice, even if they weren't all that happy about it. They knew she was leaving, and they couldn't stop her.

Knowing she had made the right choice, Deidre attended New York University the following fall.

While she still worried that her parents didn't understand this was the best thing for her, she absolutely loved it!

Being able to walk everywhere in the city, the hustle and bustle of city life—it all reached a special place in her soul. She loved seeing the sights every weekend. She made a ton of new friends.

Deidre made sure to go home every holiday and major break. She FaceTimed with her parents every morning on the way to class and let them know how she was doing on her tests and assignments. FaceTime allowed her parents to see her campus and to see that she was safe.

In six years, (four for the bachelor's degree and two for the master's degree), Deidre finished school.

When looking for a job, she needed to look for a place to settle down and raise a family.

She couldn't think of a better place than her hometown.

She moved ten minutes away from her parents and is now a school counselor at the same high school she went to.

Now, Ms. Hall and Deidre are co-workers and friends.

With her paychecks, Deidre is able help her parents financially, just like they helped her when she was young. She knows that one day, when she gets married and has children, having her mom and dad close will be a blessing.

Deidre will never forget the sacrifice her parents made by letting her go away to school. She thanks her lucky stars every day that they loved her enough to let her fly away and make her own way in the world.

Deidre's parents are so proud of the woman she has become. They are thrilled that she chose to come back home.

After all, "La familia lo es todo!"

Chapter 4

LUKE'S STORY

The blood-curdling scream pierces my dream. Crazy. There it is again. I sit up in bed. There it is again…only this time, I am wide awake; it sounds like my mom screaming. What the…?

I jump out of bed and run into the living room. There, I see two policemen. I look at my mom who has fallen to the floor. She is crying with her hands over her face.

"What's going on?" I scream.

All I can hear is her screaming, "He's dead. He's dead! Your brother is dead!"

That was the night my brother, my best friend, died. It was this past summer. He got caught up in a gang fight, and I'm still numb.

I look for him in his room.

I look for him at school.

I look for him with his other friends. I can still smell him in our house.

Why him? He was everything to me. He was my hero, and we did everything together. What am I supposed to do without him? How can I move on? I am motionless, like a zombie—just a dead, empty shell going through the motions.

Everyone tells me I have to keep going, but I just don't want to.

I wish I were dead, too.

I walk into class this morning. I sit down, pull my hoodie up over my head, put my head on the desk and close my eyes. My brother is still all I can think about. Pain is all I can feel.

"Luke!" My teacher yells.

I open my eyes but don't move. I stay sitting here with my head down. None of this matters. Nothing matters. We're all just going through the motions until we die. It's inevitable. Why care? I wish death would come sooner rather than later. At least I'd be with my brother again.

My teacher, Mr. Jones, quietly comes to my desk. So quietly, I don't even hear him. He gets down on my level and looks me in the eye. I feel like he can see me, all the way into my soul. He sees my pain, the suffering and everything in between.

I close my eyes.

I don't want him to see me. I don't want to let anyone in. It feels good to wrap my anger and sadness around me like a thick, warm blanket.

He says, very softly, "Luke, let's take a walk outside."

I'd love to say, "No, thank you," but I can see that he won't let me off so easily. I might as well give in. I don't have the strength to fight him.

He takes me outside the classroom and says, "I see a student who used to get good grades and had a light in his eyes. I see a student who used to participate and seemed to enjoy school. I see a student who used to hang out with his friends. Now, when I see you, the light in your eyes is gone. It's vanished. I see that you've stopped washing your hair. I see that when you come into class, you shut everyone out and put your head down. I see you sitting by yourself and not eating when I monitor at lunchtime. I see someone who used to fight for their education and their life now looking like they have given up entirely. I just wanted to ask you," again, he looks at me and really SEES me. "Are you okay?"

He looks extremely genuine in his question—like he's really worried about me and how I am feeling.

This catches me off guard.

I thought he was going to yell at me like my English teacher did when she was upset that I had so many missing assignments. I was prepared for a lecture, not compassion.

We stand in silence. I keep waiting for him to say more, to fill the increasing gap of awkward silence. But he doesn't.

He lets the silence sit.

The compassion and empathy in his eyes break through my walls, and I start crying. "I'm not okay. I'm not okay at all. My brother died over the summer. And I don't want to be here any longer either. He was everything to me. Now with my everything gone, there is nothing left to live for."

Mr. Jones puts his hand on my shoulder. It is both reassuring and comforting; it lets me know I am not alone. He looks at me with kindness and understanding.

It feels good to tell someone what I am going through. I thought it would be terrible, but I suddenly feel like I have someone to share this unbearable load with. There's less weight on me.

Mr. Jones says, "I have never lost a brother before. I cannot imagine the pain you are going through right now. I do know what it is like to lose someone you love very much. I was the first person in my family to go to college. My grandmother helped raise me. Of all the people who were proud of me, she was the proudest. She was very poor, and she was so proud that someone in her family was going to make it big in her lifetime.

"When I was in college, she was diagnosed with cancer. She died a few months before my graduation. I was crushed. For the first time ever, my grades were slipping.

I did so poorly on a test right after her passing that my professor pulled me aside and asked if I was okay. I told him that I didn't know if college was worth it anymore. Without my grandma, nothing was worth it. The point was to make her proud, but she isn't here anymore, so what was the point?

"My professor told me, 'The point is to STILL make her proud. She wouldn't want you to give up your big goals and dreams just because she passed away. She wouldn't want to see you fail tests because you were sad. She would want you to achieve your goals and have the tenacity to make it through. She would want you to never give up, ESPECIALLY not because of her. She wanted you to succeed. YOU should want you to succeed as well.'"

Mr. Jones looks at me proudly. "And succeed I did. As I walked the stage on that graduation day, I knew that somehow, somewhere my grandma was cheering for me in the loudest way that only she could. As I received my diploma, I thought, We did it, Grandma! We did it!"

Mr. Jones has tears in his eyes. He is thinking back on that special day in real-time. "Luke," he says quietly, "I don't think your brother would want you to give up. He was your hero. Would your hero want you to give up everything you loved and have worked so hard for your whole life?"

I shake my head no.

Mr. Jones continues, "OR…would he want you to live out your best life, in a way he will never be able to?"

I start sobbing again—I can't help it. "You're right," I say. "He would want me to achieve all of my goals, to keep playing basketball and graduate high school. He wouldn't want to see me sad. He'd be really mad at me if I gave up. He would give me hell about it." I smile a little, the first smile in a long time, thinking about the talk my brother would be giving me if he were here right now.

Mr. Jones smiles too. "Make your brother proud. But also make YOURSELF proud. It's what he would've wanted. We have a grief counselor at our school. I'm going to give him your name, so he can help you through the grieving process. You have a big life to live, and I KNOW you will give your brother lots to celebrate as you live it."

I nod, and we head back to class. I hope the counselor can help because even though Mr. Jones may be right, and even though I feel better talking to him, I am just not sure. The pain is still so deep…

LIFE HAPPENS

You have learned about tenacity, and it all sounds great…right up to a time in your life when something happens, something big.

It has the potential to derail you. You find yourself wanting to give up.

You didn't plan on this event happening, but it did. Now you feel defeated.

COVID was a good example. Teens lost their sports seasons, proms and graduation ceremonies…not to mention loved ones. COVID wasn't a planned event. It just happened. You had to distance-learn from home, you missed your friends and the support they gave you.

Life happens.

WHAT'S IN YOUR BACKPACK?

We all carry an invisible backpack filled with our life experiences. These experiences—and how we handle them—make up who we are. It's so important to remember that *everyone*, not just you, has some-thing they struggle with. You just may not know about it. This includes every person you know, at home and school—your teachers, your par-ents, your friends.

Everyone. They all have a backpack they carry every day. Inside it is something they are dealing with and trying to overcome.

Your backpack contains good experiences, fun times, all the people you love, your grandma, your brothers, sisters and parents. But it's also full of things you *struggle with*, things that can tear down tenacity.

Most teens struggle with their appearance.

"I'm too short… I'm too tall… My nose is too big."

Did you know your height, your nose and your appearance are genetic? This means you have NO control over them. There are also many other common uncontrollable issues teens struggle with.

Here are a few.

ADD (attention-deficit disorder) or ADHD (attention-deficit hyperactivity disorder: Some teens have ADD or ADHD. They get easily distracted and find it really hard to focus at school. Homework is tough because when teens are on their own, they can find it challenging to focus without a teacher standing over them.

Dyslexia: Some teens have dyslexia in their backpacks. Dyslexia doesn't always just mean they flip-flop letters and numbers. Dyslexia makes it hard to study. It is hard to "read between the lines" and keep information in their heads long enough to take the test the next day.

Dyslexia makes taking tests even harder for teens who also have test anxiety. They may have studied last night, but when they sit down to take the test, all the information leaves their brains. Their ability to recall what they studied is harder, which is why it's such a big challenge to carry in their backpacks.

Tourette's Syndrome: Tourette's syndrome is where someone has twitches and tics they can't control. Teens might be on medicines to help them control the tics at school. But these medicines can make them feel tired and gain weight. Many teens with Tourette's syndrome get teased at school for something they can't control, and this all lives in their backpacks.

If you have ADD, ADHD, dyslexia or Tourette's syndrome, does it mean you'll never reach your dreams, never go to college? No! It just means you are going to have to work twice as hard as someone without as many backpack issues.

Like Luke, some teens have dark, suicidal thoughts in their backpacks. It's hard being a teen, but SUICIDE IS NEVER AN OPTION.

Let me say it again, suicide is NEVER an option.

Tell somebody if you are thinking about suicide! Tell a trusted teacher, your counselor, a parent, an aunt or uncle. Reach out and get help.

Make an agreement with your friends that if suicide EVER crosses your mind, you will reach out to them first. If your friend reaches out to you, don't keep it a secret. Go with your friend to tell their trusted adult on campus.

There is a hotline number for suicide prevention:

This number reaches the Suicide and Crisis Lifeline, a safe and confidential place to find help. You can also find this number and other help at their website: **988lifeline.org**.

If you are reading this and thinking about suicide, call **988** and reach out for help.

If your friend is thinking about suicide, help them call **988**.

You can even chat with them online: **988lifeline.org**.

You have goals and dreams. You are going to make a difference in this world. The world needs you.

Suicide is never an option.

STRESS AND TEEN TENACITY

Teens certainly have a lot to deal with in their backpacks. Any of these can trip you up and take you off course.

The trick to life is knowing what issues are in your backpack and figuring out which ones are little (1s or 2s), which are serious—but not urgent (5s or 6s), and which ones are 10s. If we can't figure that out, your backpack will become heavier and heavier over time.

How do you tell the difference?

THINK ABOUT IT:

Imagine a box with four squares inside of it.

Each square is a small box with a label: Box 1, Box 2, Box 3, and Box 4. When problems come at you during the day, don't carry them in your backpack. Instead, put each problem into the correct box.

Box 1: Is this an emergency?

Do I drop everything I'm doing to handle this problem, right now? Do I deal with my friend's issue immediately? Do I stop following my goals and address this problem? Do I let it take me off track?

So, what's an emergency?

Is my house on fire? Yes! That's an emergency.

You have a book report due at the end of the month. Is that an emergency? No, that is something you can plan for.

Box 2: Can it wait until after school?

My friend needs me to help right now. She is having troubles with her boyfriend.

Ask yourself, "Can this wait until after school?" If it can, put it into box 2 instead of in your backpack.

Can you write it down on a piece of paper to remind yourself to get to it after school?

Can you write it on your hand, so you don't forget?

Can it wait?

Box 3: Can I get help?

When life is coming at you, fast and furious, it is really easy to get overwhelmed (tight chest, fast heartbeat) and want to give up.

Box 3 is where you reach out and get help.

If you hate Algebra, don't understand it and your grades are dropping…get some help.

The school may have tutors to help you at lunch. The teacher may even be willing to offer extra help if you are stuck.

If you don't reach out, no one knows you are struggling.

Teens with tenacity put their appropriate struggles into box 3, and then they seek the help they need.

Box 4: I'll do it later.

I hear it all month when the book report is coming due. "I'll do it later. I have plenty of time."

Remember the book, *Great Expectations*, which has 550 pages? If you put reading that book into box 4, you will end up reading 4-5 hours a day that last week before it's due.

It's not going to happen!

Instead, plan it out in little chunks over time.

What issues are you struggling with now that you are carrying in your backpack? Write them down in the corresponding boxes below.

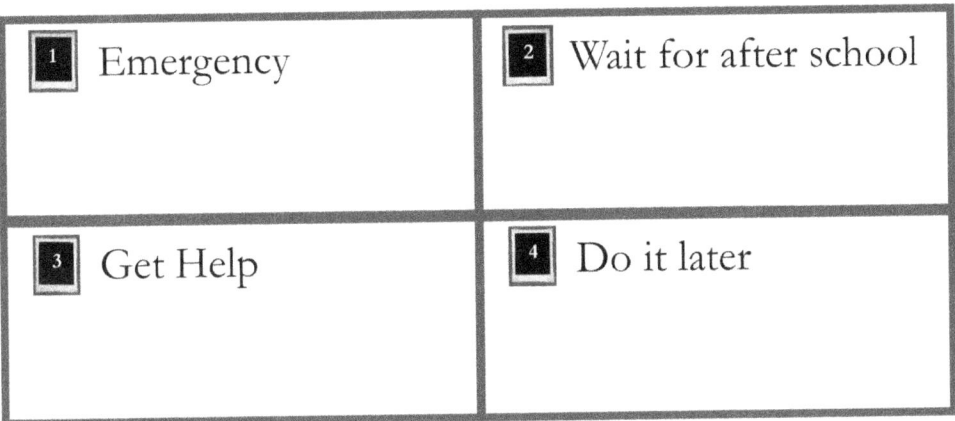

In which box do most adults put everything? Usually, they put it into box 1, where it's an emergency…the kids, the bills, the job, the car. This isn't healthy, and it's one reason why your parents get so stressed.

In which box do you think most teens put everything?

Most teens live in box 4! They say, "I'll do it later…" but later never happens.

Time has a way of slipping away from all of us. The school year starts, and before you know it, it's Christmas. The next thing you know, the year is over.

Limit what you put into box 4 because *later* never comes.

TIME MANAGEMENT

How are you going to have the tenacity to go after your dreams if everything is sitting in your "later" box? This box just builds and builds until everything comes due, and you are overwhelmed.

Almost everything in your "later" box can be handled with good time management.

Time management includes making a plan to get the homework done.

When you first sit down on Monday to tackle homework, take the first 15 minutes to organize yourself.

Write this down on paper:
1. What is due tomorrow?
2. What is due Friday?
3. What is due later in the month?

To help keep organized, get a big, wall-sized calendar. Write down when things are due. You don't want to walk into class today and hear, "Your book report is due today."

When you write your plan and due dates down on paper, it takes them out of your head—and out of your backpack! All these little details won't be rolling around in your head, and that means one less stressball you have to juggle tonight when you go to bed.

Teens with tenacity know what's due, and they organize their time to make sure it gets done.

TIME SUCKERS

Time suckers are all those things you do that steal time away from you without you even realizing it. What are some typical time suckers in a teen's life?

Gaming: How long can a gamer game? Having raised three gamer boys, they can game through breakfast, lunch and dinner. They don't even feel hungry when they are "into" their game.

They lose all track of time and suddenly realize they've been at it for hours.

Social Media: Have you ever said, "Let me sit here and check out TikTok just to relax for a minute," then deeper and deeper you go until you start feeling tired?

Four hours down the Internet hole without realizing it…and now you are too exhausted to do homework!

"I'll do it later…"

THINK ABOUT IT:

Scrolling through TikTok videos to relax a bit is not the problem. Being a gamer is not the problem.

The only problem is the amount of time you SPEND on these activities!

Solution: Set the timer on your phone for 30 minutes.

Enjoy your time gaming and scrolling through Instagram or TikTok. When the timer goes off, shut down the game or social media, and get back to homework.

Make a contract with yourself that rewards you for getting the homework done: I'll study for an hour, then play games for 30 minutes.

Teens with tenacity set that timer as a way to keep themselves focused.

EMOTIONS AND TEEN TENACITY

What else can pull you away from tenacity? Emotions can trip you up—and teens have a lot of them (as do adults).

Emotions are a natural part of life. The issue is when people allow them to dictate what they will do. They get mad and act out. They get sad and withdraw. They get happy and forget their responsibilities.

Of course, all these emotions are normal. And it's okay to feel them! What is NOT appropriate is ACTING out on them. Acting out on your emotions without stepping back and thinking them through is never okay.

Experts encourage us to recognize that emotions are not what we **are**; they are something we **have**.

They are also **temporary**.

The next time you think, *I'm so mad! I'm sad*, change those thoughts to the correct ones:

I ***feel*** *so mad!*

I ***feel*** *sad.*

Then, step back and think about what you are feeling. Don't act out on the emotion in the heat of the moment. These feelings and emotions are temporary, and they pass. Once they do, you can see clearly and then decide what to do.

THINK ABOUT IT:

You turn the corner and see your girlfriend flirting with your friend. Unbelievable! There they are, just the two of them talking. The way she is laughing looks like they are flirting.

Your emotions start to take over, your heart starts racing faster, you don't think. You walk right over there and start yelling in the hall, accusing them of being a couple. They try to explain they were just talking while waiting for you, but you can't stop. You are seeing red. You are jealous and ready to fight.

Your emotions have taken over.

The second you start to feel your emotions overtake you, **STOP**!

Think for a moment.

Ask yourself, *Am I jumping to conclusions? Could there be a reasonable explanation?*

Realize this emotion of jealousy will pass once you hear the explanation. Step back, take a breath, and think it through. Remember, emotions are something you have; they are not who you are.

WHAT CAUSES CRAZY EMOTIONS?

Emotions can be all over the place. You may feel happy one minute, then sad and crying the next, then worried, then depressed, then rage... all within an hour or even minutes.

Why?

Three big reasons for crazy emotions are diet, not getting enough sleep and overthinking.

Let's look at your diet.

What are you eating? *Well, for breakfast I had an Oreo and a cup of coffee. After school, I ate the rest of the pack of Oreos, and washed it down with another cup of coffee.* This kind of diet will put you right next to the edge, just waiting for a little gray snake to push you over.

Not getting enough sleep?

Sleep resets your mind and body to prepare for each day. Going to sleep way too late and then having to get up all too early can result in you not getting the deep sleep that your brain desperately needs to function properly. Lack of sleep can really mess with your emotions.

Maybe you are overthinking situations and blowing them out of proportion.

You feel this big buildup of all these overwhelming emotions, and you keep dwelling on and reliving them...and it's exhausting. Overthinking any situation does no good.

No matter what causes big feelings, when your emotions flare, step back and look at the bigger picture. Remember that having emotions is normal. Let yourself feel them but know they don't define you, and they will pass.

Step back, take a deep breath, and give yourself time to rationally think through the situation.

I'M LONELY

Everyone needs friends. We need to feel loved and connected to others. But…who are your friends? Sometimes, we become friends with people and put up with things they do that bring us down. This is an unhealthy friendship and might be one of those things you are adding to your backpack.

Do your friends bring you UP or do they bring you DOWN? Do they make you a better person? Or are your friends putting you down? Are they posting negative things about you? Do you trust them with your secrets, or do you have to keep your guard up around them?

Do they make you feel better, or do they make you feel stressed with their drama, drama, drama?

Choose your friends wisely. If you are allowing them to control and impact your emotions, they really are not a good friend. Don't allow them to do this to you. Pick friends who build you up, not tear you down just to make themselves look better.

HOMEWORK:

1. What's in your backpack that you struggle with?

2. Go back to the boxes you filled out on page 99. What items can be moved into more appropriate boxes?

3. What is your #1, biggest time sucker?

SELF-REFLECTION:

Put what is stressing you in the box where it belongs. Not everything is an emergency, and not everything can be done later. Some challenges require help. Don't act on your emotions. Remember, emotions are not who you are but rather, they are how you feel. Step back and think things through before acting. Watch out for the time-suckers in life. Stay focused. Keep your goals in mind. Practice tenacity.

TIPS FOR TEACHERS:

Students are going through so much that we teachers have no idea about. Before we rush to judge or get mad or frustrated with students for not completing their assignments, it is important to look for key signs to see if their mental health is okay.

Mr. Jones noticed that Luke had a sudden shift in behavior and personality. This was a telltale sign that something was not right. Luke showed several signs of depression (his hair not being washed, lost joy for things he previously loved doing, good grades turning into poor grades, etc.), and while teachers are not doctors and cannot diagnose, we are on the front lines every day. We see our students the most.

When we notice big shifts, it is important to ask, genuinely and with compassion, if they are okay. Then, let the silence sit. Most of the time, the student will let their emotions come to the surface and will confide in us.

More than we realize, many of our students experience death and are grieving. Teachers can let them know about a time when we were going through something similar and how we overcame that hardship. This can be very helpful. Sharing our experiences allows students to know that they are not alone in these feelings and that overcoming this hardship is very possible.

It is important to let the counselor know what is going on so that we can put our students into the hands of a mental health professional or get them the resources the counselor can provide.

COUNSELOR'S THOUGHTS:

Grief is a tricky emotion that many students do not know how to navigate. It is a combination of sadness, anger, regret and confusion at the realization of no longer having "that" person in your life.

Grief is not like happiness where it washes over you and can be felt radiating off you. Grief is commonly associated with a feeling of being crushed by a wave. It comes and goes. It is up and down…completely sweeping you up into its current, only to throw you back onto the beach, battered and alone.

I often have students ask me how long it will be until they feel "better." The truth is, grief can naturally last anywhere from six months to *years*. Unfortunately, this is not the answer they are looking for.

Grief needs an outlet. Encourage students experiencing grief to talk, write, dance, draw, scream, sing, and work out to help them process and release their grief.

As counselors, it is our job to help students see what they are carrying in their backpacks and help them understand their complex feelings. Our job is also to offer students a safe space and provide the necessary support to help them continue their education despite what life throws at them.

Mr. Jones is the perfect reminder of why it's also important to set up "Handle with Care" training in your school.

He is a great example of the difference a teacher can make when they have the opportunity and empathy to "handle" their students "with care." He had no idea what was going on in Luke's personal life, but he noticed a change in behavior, work, and motivation.

Instead of acting on his frustration over Luke not being a "good student," Mr. Jones was able to step back and think. He was able to use his training to help him choose to try to understand Luke and better connect on the student's level.

This allowed him to really see what Luke had in his backpack that was weighing him down.

The "Handle with Care" approach allows staff to see teens as unique individuals who are struggling with real-life experiences.

Like Luke, some teens have a heavier backpack than others.

Other common problems teens carry in their backpacks include:

✓ My parents are getting a divorce. All they do is fight and yell at each other. My stomach is always in knots, and I don't want to go home.

✓ My parents have two jobs, and I'm expected to raise my brothers and sisters, as well as myself. I have to wake them up every morning, get them dressed and fed, walk them to school, and then walk myself to school. I'm only 14.

✓ My mom has cancer. She needs me. I clean up after the chemo makes her sick. How can I leave her and go off to college? I'm watching her wither away. What will I do without my mom?

Counselors can offer these students access to services they would not otherwise have access to. They are called "Wrap-Around Services." These resources might be through the district or a school-affiliated mental health partnership. They allow students like Luke to receive therapy services at school while also providing an opportunity for the same therapist to work with the rest of his family at home in a group setting.

Counselors can help keep a student like Luke grounded and feeling safe while he is on campus. Find out who his "trusted adult" is, and make sure he checks in with them weekly. This could be the student's favorite teacher, coach or a campus supervisor. It could be any adult who makes the student feel like they are "really being seen" and safe.

As counselors, we need to help all staff understand that they may be that one safe adult their students are looking for to help lighten their load. Teens and adults should never label themselves by what is in their backpacks. We all have something that we are dealing with.

Tenacity means limiting what is going into your backpack and learning how to deal with what is in there. As counselors, we can help our teachers support our students in developing tenacity.

LUKE'S OUTCOME:

Luke had all but given up on life. He was pushing everyone away. His grief was pulling him under…fast. Mr. Jones referred him to the counselor who was able to set up "Wrap-Around Services" for Luke and his family.

This support helped him begin to manage his grief.

Luke started working hard again. He did his best to make his brother AND himself proud because he realized they both deserved nothing less. He continued playing basketball, his favorite sport to play with his brother.

Every time his team won a game, Luke sent a silent, "We did it!" to his brother.

When Luke graduated high school, he was sad for a moment when he saw just his mom and dad in the audience, and his brother was missing. But then he looked up at the sky and KNEW that somehow, some way, his brother was watching and cheering him on.

Luke had succeeded in making his brother and himself proud!

He decided to enroll in trade school to become an auto mechanic. Working on cars was something he and his brother had liked to do for fun. Those skills he had learned from his brother would now help Luke put food on the table for his family, while also keeping his brother's memory alive.

Chapter 5

OLIVIA'S STORY

In 6th grade, I decided I was going to be popular. I'd been shy all my life. I had no friends. I was never noticed. I felt invisible. I studied the popular girls, how they laughed and walked, how they brushed the hair out of their eyes, how they shook their heads. I watched as they flirted with boys. I wanted to be just like them and decided that I'd do anything to become one of them. I practiced being a popular girl at night in my room when no one was watching.

At the start of 7th grade, I cut my hair, got rid of my glasses and changed my looks so that I would look like Emily. Emily was so pretty. Everybody liked her and followed her around. I would do anything to be her friend. She had never been nice to me, but maybe now that I cut my hair and looked like her, she would notice me. Maybe we could be friends.

Emily did notice me and included me in her group. She always asked me to get her milk at lunch and to throw away her trash. She even wanted me to do her homework for her, but at least I was with the popular girls.

I heard others in Emily's group talk about how evil Emily could be if she didn't really like you. But I wasn't worried about that. I was willing to do whatever it took to be friends with Emily, so I could be popular.

That all changed on a rainy Wednesday morning…

Mom slows the car down to drop me off at school. Looking out the window, I see this large crowd of kids gathered out front. I get out of the car and immediately notice that everyone is pointing at me and laughing.

What the heck?

I quickly look down at my clothes. Did I spill food on my shirt? Is my skirt tucked into my underwear? Is there something in my teeth?

Nope. There's nothing wrong with my clothes and nothing in my teeth, so what's so funny? I don't get it.

Still, I hold my head up high and start towards class. Everyone is following me and laughing their heads off. My face is red. Why is this happening? I don't under-stand what's going on…

Then, Emily comes up to me with a huge smile on her face.

She whips out her phone and proudly shows me a picture of me on social media and…

I taste vomit coming up…

OMG! It's a picture of my face but it is connected to a very naked woman's body!

I feel like someone just punched me in the gut, everything is clenching up. My head starts thumping.

"Whose body is that?" I ask.

Emily smiles at me and says, "Why, it's YOUR body, is it not?"

Her smile is so wicked as she gives me a sideways glance. She smiles at the crowd, bringing them all into the joke. She looks like a cat that has just caught a huge rat.

I get it now. The joke is me!

This isn't funny.

"WHAT are you talking about?" I demand. "THAT is not my body!"

She looks at me coyly and says, "Of course it is, silly. You posed for pictures at my house, remember?"

"I most certainly did not!" I angrily yell at her.

"Come on now, Olivia. Don't you remember? You BEGGED me to take pictures of you naked and post them on social media for your crush to see."

I'm seeing red. Hot anger is flooding through my veins. "Emily, you KNOW I did NO such thing!" I say loudly so all can hear. "Why are you doing this? I thought we were friends!"

Emily laughed and shook her head. "I don't know what you are talking about," she says. "Why would I want to be friends with you?"

I catch my breath and feel the color draining from my face.

Emily fake-smiles sweetly at me…the back-stabbing b*tch that she is! She knows what she has done. She obviously took a picture of my face and Photoshopped it onto a naked body. Then she posted it!

For all the world to see!

Forever!

My life is over!

This will never go away.

I wish I could disappear forever.

I run to the bathroom, close the stall door and cry as quietly as I can. What is happening? I changed who I was. I did everything Emily wanted to make her like me and be my friend.

Why would she do this?

I hate her! Now, I see she is not my friend. Was she ever?

I feel so alone. I don't want to be here in this world. There's no way to fix this. Nowhere to escape the embarrassment.

I feel so alone and so ashamed.

When mom picks me up after school, I start bawling. Today was too much to bear.

"Help me, Mom," I say after telling her everything. "Tell me we can fix this. That it will all go away. I don't want to live with this following me forever."

Mom looks at me and pats my head. "Don't worry about it honey," she says condescendingly. "Just forget about it, and it will all go away."

"WHAT?" I ask, completely astonished. "What do you mean, it will all go away? It's all over school, social media, the Internet! It will NOT just go away! This is the WORST thing that could EVER happen!"

"Well! Aren't you being a tad dramatic, dear?" she asks. "Mark my words… Tomorrow everyone will forget about it, and everything will go back to normal."

We pull up to the house, and Mom jumps out of the car like it's nothing. Like my life, my reputation and the loss of my friend is NOTHING.

Do I matter so little to her?

She clearly does not care about me. Emily, who I thought was my friend, obviously does not care about me. My dad left when I was little and never came back. He never cared about me.

So why, then, should I care about myself?

As this horrible day finally ends, I climb into bed.

But I don't want to sleep. That means tomorrow will get here sooner. And Mom is so wrong. This isn't just going to go away. It's not going to be better tomorrow. There's no way out of this.

I still can't believe Mom's attitude. I can't believe she doesn't care that I was so humiliated.

No one cares about my life.

Again, I wonder why I should care about my life, either.

This will embarrass me forever. My life is ruined. It will NEVER get better. I don't want to live in a world where nothing will EVER get better.

All I want to do is end it.

There is no hope.

The next few days pass by in a blur. Everyone still makes fun of me. I don't bother talking about it with Mom anymore. I can't eat. I lay in bed each night worrying about each day to come. The torment is overwhelming, the loneliness unbearable.

I just don't want to be here anymore...

As the weeks pass, I am so exhausted that I start sleeping during my classes. My grades are falling from all As to all Fs. I'm not okay, and Mom doesn't even notice. No one does.

I'm pretty sure no one would notice if I wasn't here anymore. Clearly, no one cares about me. Why should I? It's time to do something about it.

Today, I fall asleep during science. My teacher, Mr. Billings, wakes me up and asks, "Olivia, are you awake?"

I raise my head up expecting to see an angry teacher glaring down at me. His anger would be understandable.

I don't care though. This is just one more reason why the world doesn't need me. I'm a useless student, a useless person.

But it doesn't matter.

I won't be here much longer anyway.

I made a plan to leave this life this afternoon, after school, so nothing else that happens today matters.

I am surprised though.

Mr. Billings is down on my level. When I look into his eyes, I see kindness and compassion. This isn't what I was expecting.

He asks, "Can I see you outside the classroom for a moment, please?"

I follow him outside, and he says, "I've noticed a change in you lately. You are normally an A student, but you have not turned in any work in the past three weeks. I noticed you are sleeping more during the day, which tells me that you are not getting enough sleep at night. I've noticed it's been a while since you last showered or groomed yourself. I just want to ask you, are you okay?"

I wait for him to say more.

But he doesn't.

He's just silent.

I shift uncomfortably, not wanting to talk to him. Surely, he'll start back up lecturing me and end this silence...

But he doesn't.

He's just calmly, silently, waiting for me to answer.

I look in his eyes. He seems so genuine. I feel like he understands me, like he sees me. Right down to my very soul. I believe he is actually worried about me.

Someone cares, *I think*. Someone notices that I am not okay.

He still doesn't say anything more. We just stand here in that awkward silence.

But his eyes are saying: "I'm here for you. I will wait for you to talk."

I can't help it.

The silence.

The compassion on his face.

The fact that SOMEONE *notices that I am feeling awful and alone, like I don't matter.*

The silence is too much. The caring is too strong. I start sobbing and sobbing and can't stop.

Everything I have been feeling is laying bare.

I shake my head. "I'm not okay," I say even though I'm scared he might just blow it off and tell me I'm being dramatic.

"I can see that," he tells me. "I'm here for you. I see you. You matter. I hope you know that." And his eyes say it all. He cares.

I believe him, and I sob harder. "Well, that makes one person."

"Olivia, I care about you. All of your teachers care about you. We've all been worried about you. You are one of our best students." He suddenly gets very serious and says, "I need to make sure you're okay, for your safety. I will never forgive myself if something happens to you… Have you been having suicidal thoughts?"

I look at him, shocked. How could he possibly know about my plan?

Today's plan…?

Mr. Billings continues, "I'm not a doctor, but a lot of the changes I've seen in you are signs of depression. I'm going to take you to the counselor to talk about how you are doing. They can assess you and possibly get you resources and help.

"I know sometimes it seems like no one cares, and you might think that the world is a better place without you. But those thoughts are not correct. I just want you to know that you MATTER. This world needs you. The world is a better place because YOU are in it. I also want you to know that you are NOT alone. Remember that. I'm here to help you and so is the counselor. Whatever problems you are going through are temporary. Do not make a permanent decision for a temporary problem."

We head to the counselor's office. I know he means well, but teachers are supposed to care or at least try to, aren't they? What about Mom? What about my friends?

As we walk, I can't stop thinking about Emily and what she did. I thought she was my friend. I changed who I was and how I looked to make her like me and be my friend. I don't even know who I am anymore...

I just don't see how a counselor can help.

"WHO ARE YOU?"

All teens struggle with their identity. They struggle with finding their voice and their place in the world.

Being a teen with tenacity means you do not have to go with the flow and follow what your friends want you to do.

You don't have to be quiet just because that is what your friend wants. You don't have to be a drinker because your friends are drinking.

Being a teen with tenacity means finding out who you are, choosing what you want to do with your life and creating a plan to get you there.

YOUR ELEVATOR SPEECH

In high school, you'll probably start looking for a job. You'll have to fill out applications and go to job interviews.

You may also start filling out college admission applications, writing your personal statement, and applying for volunteer opportunities.

The first question everyone will ask you is, "Tell me a little bit about yourself. Who are you?"

Having a prepared elevator speech ready is just as important as dressing to impress.

WHAT IS AN ELEVATOR SPEECH?

Imagine you are stepping onto the elevator of a 12-story building to go to a job or college interview.

Now imagine that the owner of the company or the university admissions representative gets on the elevator with you.

They turn and look at you and say, "Hey, I'm Jess. Who are you?"

Well, who are you?

You have ten seconds (the time it takes the elevator to go up those twelve floors) to impress them and tell them all about who you are. You have an opportunity to show them what you value, your goals, and what makes you different from everyone else they will meet today.

Do you have your elevator speech ready?

I've worked with teens over the past ten years and have asked them, "Who are you?"

Most teens have never thought about it.

There was one time though, when I had a 16-year-old stand up and say, "Hi. My name is Daniel, and I play football. I like science, and I want to go to college to become a biology teacher. I love my family, and I have good friends. I enjoy life."

Now, that's a teen with an elevator speech!

HOW TO CREATE
YOUR ELEVATOR SPEECH

Creating your elevator speech takes some self-reflection. This means thinking about what you value, what you feel is important in life, and what you want to become.

Start by thinking about your character.

✓ How do you look to others? How do you come across to your friends? Do they see you as a person who follows through on what you promised you would do? What do you bring to your friendships?

✓ What traits do you value in people? Do you value honesty? Is it important to you that people keep their word? Are there things that your friends do that you *don't* like? What characteristics have you seen in other people that bother you?

✓ What do you believe in? What things are important to you? What are your goals?

Now, ask yourself, "What do I want to become in life?"

Some teens know what they want to be in life and can immediately tell you, "I want to be a teacher… I want to be a nurse…"

One teen told me, "I want to own my own Mickey D's." (McDonald's.)

I loved it. "That's called being an entrepreneur," I told him. "That is creating your own path, your own destiny."

That teen will learn how to run a business and be successful on his own. He has a goal, a dream and the tenacity to get there.

Other teens have to think long and hard about what they want to do with their lives. I've had some just give me a blank stare when I ask what they want to do with their life. They just shrug their shoulders and say, "I don't know."

In one middle school, I noticed a 14-year-old sleeping with her head on the desk.

I went over to her and asked, "How about you? What do you want to do in life?"

She lifted her head long enough to look me in the eye and say, "I want to be a vet. You know, an animal doctor." Then, she put her head back down on the desk and went back to sleep.

Huh??

So, I asked her, "How do you plan on achieving that goal in life?"

"I don't know," she groaned. "I'll worry about it when I'm a senior." And back to sleep, she went.

Do you think she will make it? Does she show tenacity?

Nope!

If she waits to start until her senior year, it may be too late for her to get there. As you've learned, by senior year, you need to be about done.

INTERVIEWING FOR YOUR FIRST JOB

When you go out to look for your first job, possible employers are going to ask you how much experience you have. Many teens get stuck here.

They think, *I don't have any experience because this will be my first job, and that's where I get experience.*

Use your tenacity here. Tell the person interviewing you all about the volunteer work you've done. Show them how you've learned to work with others, how you showed up on time and learned to be responsible.

When you go out looking for that first job emphasize these points:

✓ I have a lot of volunteer EXPERIENCE.

✓ I have PRIDE in what I do.

✓ I am MOTIVATED to do the best job I can.

✓ I am a teen with TENACITY.

Remember, volunteering gives you the opportunity to work with others. It also teaches you how to network and how to find out what really interests you.

Volunteering somewhere might light a fire in your soul that could change your life. It can help you picture yourself in a certain career, enjoying life doing something you love to do.

Volunteering also shows your future boss, college, or trade school that you are working towards your goals.

Volunteering shows that you have tenacity.

THINK ABOUT IT:

If you aren't working TOWARDS a goal, you are floating. You are floating through the day, aimlessly going in whatever direction the wind blows or your friends take you. Floating means following along with everyone else, following their way, their path, their goals.

Don't float! Don't just take things that come at you.
Don't just accept whatever life has in store for you.

Make YOUR path.
Have tenacity.
Dream it.
Do it.

FEELING OVERWHELMED

Do you sometimes feel like you're playing the game of whack-a-mole? You are trying and trying but things just aren't going your way. It gets like that sometimes in life, and we all have to learn to roll with it. How do you do that? By using some solid coping skills that help you handle the rough patches until they pass.

Here are three tips to practice when you find yourself feeling overwhelmed:

1. Don't sweat the small stuff
2. Don't run your misfortunes over and over in your head
3. Get what's bothering you out of your head.

DON'T SWEAT THE SMALL STUFF

I love this expression because it says, "Don't worry about all the little 1s and 2s on your stress ruler."

Remember, all those little things can build up and overwhelm you if you are treating them like they are 10s. Little things usually get bigger and bigger when you start overthinking and worrying about them all night.

So, "Don't sweat the small stuff..." The other half of that expression is: "And it's **ALL** small stuff!"

DON'T RUN YOUR PROBLEMS
OVER AND OVER IN YOUR HEAD

You had a fight with your friend at school today, and it upset you. Then, the teacher got on you for not turning in your homework. You went home and told your mom about it, getting all upset when you described the day to her. Then, you called your other friend, told him all about it and got even more upset talking about it again.

You went to bed and couldn't sleep because every time you thought about the day, you got upset, and you kept going over it and juggling it in your head.

THINK ABOUT IT:

Imagine you have a lemon tree in your backyard. You go outside and pick a fresh, juicy lemon right off the tree. You take it in the house and cut it in half. You give it a good squeeze and the lemon juice squirts out. Now, you bring this juicy lemon up to your mouth and take a big lick.

Wow, ugh, sour! Can you feel the saliva in your mouth just from *thinking* about it? Your body reacts to what you are thinking about.

When you keep replaying your problems over and over in your head, and you constantly think and talk about those problems, your body goes into stress mode every single time. This can cause anxiety, exhaustion, and even depression.

Tell one person about it, then let it go.

GET IT OUT OF YOUR HEAD

Sometimes when you start feeling overwhelmed and it feels like more and more is being dumped on you, you just can't shut your mind off. Getting these worries out of your head may help you turn off your mind.

A good way to get it out of your head is to put it on paper.

✓ Make a list of everything you are worrying about. ALL of it. All the 1s and 2s, and even the 10s.

✓ Make a list of everything that is coming due. ALL of it. Get it out of your head and put it on paper. It's either going to rumble around in your head, or it's going to be listed on the paper.

✓ Mark each item off, one by one, after you get it finished. This will help calm your overwhelmed brain.

COPING WITH ANXIETY

Anxiety can come on fast. Your stomach starts feeling tight, and you feel shaky inside. Learn to recognize these feelings. Write the following ideas down somewhere so you can look at them when you feel anxiety coming on. It's important to have the ideas ready because it's hard to think clearly when your body starts feeling this way.

Always start by taking a deep breath. Take ten deep breaths. Focus on your breathing. Feel the air going in, feel the air going out. Each time you breathe the air out, imagine all the anxiety going out with your breath. Imagine your stomach relaxing. This will help to calm yourself down.

Walk the Dog. Your dog loves walks! Go outside and get some fresh air. If you can, walk in nature. Feel the warm sun on your face when you start to feel anxious. Or the cool wind. Pet your dog. It will help your body to calm down.

Listen to music. Get your earbuds in and listen to your favorite music. Shut the door to your room and sing out loud to the songs. Dance around. Blow off some energy. Find some upbeat songs to lift your spirits.

Get lost in a good book. Reading a good book can take your mind off your problems and your life. You can't be thinking about how bad your day was if you are into a good book. It's a great escape and a way to let your mind rest.

Journal your thoughts, doodle or draw. Use your hands to create something. Write down how you are feeling to get it out of your head. Don't just sit and overthink your worries. If you do, they will only get bigger.

Don't let worry and anxiety steal your time away from today. Time is too precious to waste.

Most people don't learn this lesson in life until it's too late.

Tomorrow is NOT a given. It's not promised to you.

It's easy to think the people in your life will never get sick or die, but it happens.

Every day teens lose family members to gangs, drugs and illness.

THINK ABOUT IT:

Maybe you've experienced an event when your mom, dad, nana or someone you love got sick. Maybe they had cancer.

Just for a minute, imagine your doctor telling you that today is your last day on earth.

Would you do anything different today after hearing this news?

Or imagine if you only had one week left to live, would you spend four hours a day on TikTok? Gaming? Would you lay around and sleep that last week away?

There is a special club of people who don't have to imagine that scenario. They live life this way. They live like every day is their last day, and they may not have a tomorrow.

This club is called: "The Cancer Club."

People who have had cancer learned this lesson of not wasting time the hard way.

I am part of this club.

I've had cancer four times and have gone through two rounds of chemo. I know my time is precious and limited, so I choose not to spend it gaming, watching TikTok videos or getting to life "later." There is no "later" for me.

Cancer is my 10.

Your mom having cancer is a 10.

This fact helps my own children put their lives into perspective. When they feel upset and overwhelmed, I always ask them to put a number on what they are feeling. My family knows, all too well, that mom having cancer is *their* 10, and nothing compares to that.

TEEN TENACITY

Being a teen with tenacity is important. **Teens with tenacity know they need determination**. Tenacity is about your life. Your goals. Your dreams. It's about writing these things down on a piece of paper and taping that paper to the bedpost, your nightstand, your mirror.

Read your goals every day.

Tenacity is also about developing your elevator speech. It's about holding on to who you are when it seems easier to imitate others.

Teens with tenacity understand that everyone they meet is struggling with something in their invisible backpack. My backpack is filled with cancer-coping skills. Yours might be filled with dyslexia, ADD, ADHD, OCD or depression.

Through volunteering, you may find others with similar issues to yours in their backpacks. This may give you the opportunity to discover how they cope…yet another great reason to volunteer!

Teens with tenacity acknowledge and remember that there are people in their lives who love them, care about them and support them. Knowing when to reach out for help is tenacity. It's the healthy side of your brain speaking out. It's also important to understand that not everyone has the skills to respond to you.

Olivia's mom did not dismiss Olivia's problems because she didn't care. It was because **she did not have the skills** to respond the way Olivia needed.

Tenacity means continuing to reach out for help even when the first person doesn't get it.

If you are struggling, I encourage you to reach out and talk to your favorite teacher, your parents, a good friend, or your counselor.

Remember, suicide is NEVER an option.

If you are thinking about suicide:

Call 988

We are all in this world together. YES! Life as a teen is often overwhelming, and teens DO have stress.

Remember there are adults who can help you.

The good news is that you are now a teen with tenacity!

You have your goals and dreams written down.

You have new coping skills you can practice to help you de-stress and find balance. It takes practice and tenacity, but you've got this, so...

Take that deep breath.

Take one step forward.

Read those goals.

Take on the world.

HOMEWORK:

1. Write your elevator speech.

2. What coping skills will you try today?

3. Are you a teen with tenacity? What tenacity traits have you developed from reading this book?

SELF-REFLECTION:

You can't control the issues given to you in your backpack. All you can control is what you **DO** with them. That's tenacity: not giving up. Practice tenacity when life gets hard.

You can do it. You are going to accomplish great things in your life. This world needs teens with tenacity, and you are one of them!

TIPS FOR TEACHERS:

Teachers see students every day. When we pay attention, we notice their big and small changes. Some of the red flags that are seen in Olivia's story are classic ones that indicate the student may not be okay. If a teacher sees these signs, it is important to ask to speak to the student away from their peers and genuinely ask if they are okay.

Once asked, the student will get very quiet. They have a lot on their mind. They are figuring out if it is safe to tell you and what, if anything, they want to express about their feelings. For many teachers, the silence that follows is hard to maintain but important. Your student needs to be the one to have time to think through their feelings.

The silence is hard for your student too. They will not be able to handle the silence and their thoughts at the same time. Not always, but most of the time, they will eventually break down and allow themselves to release their emotions, stress and mental anguish.

This is a very vulnerable and healing moment for them. After the student is done expressing their emotions, it is important to let them know that they matter. Show them that they are not alone and that you are there for them.

If there is a possibility that the student may be suicidal, it is extremely important to ask them if they have been having suicidal thoughts and if they have a plan.

Let them know you are not asking about it to get them into trouble but for their own safety. Let them know you would be devastated if anything were to happen to them. Always make sure the counselor is aware that the student is struggling with mental health, especially if they are suicidal. The counselor can assess them and take the proper steps to assist the student with their mental health. This may include therapy, one-on-one check-ins with the counselor, and doctor's referrals for possible depression and/or other mental health issues.

Teachers play one of the most important roles in helping students with their mental health. Most of the time, students do not seek out a counselor if they are going through something. They usually send signals and red flags and hope that someone, *anyone*, notices. It's their call for help when they don't feel comfortable seeking help themselves. Teachers save lives every year by reaching out to students who are showing signs of mental health struggles and getting them to the people who can help them.

COUNSELOR'S COMMENTS:

Identity is an important part of what makes a person feel safe, accepted and confident. Teenagers are just beginning to form their own identity. They are also trying on new identities to help them fit in, express themselves, and develop their own moral compass.

Students in middle and high school grapple with their identity in a multitude of ways. They start expanding their friend groups, exploring new interests, and trying on personas they believe others will like more. Sometimes, the friends, interests and personas don't gel well. Students who are struggling with their identity in order to fit in often lack the confidence or acceptance they need to be their authentic selves.

Students with strong identities are like trees with strong roots and trunks. The winds from others may shake and blow at the tree, but a teen with a strong identity stands firm in the ground, knowing who they are, down to their core.

Students who lack a strong identity (like Olivia did) are like trees with shallow roots and thin trunks. When the winds of others come barreling through, they bend easily and become uprooted with little effort.

When students stake *their entire identity* on trying to be something or someone they are not, they lose what makes them special. And if the image of their identity is challenged, cracked, or shattered, that is when they feel the most lost and alone.

Suicide and thinking about suicide are rising concerns with teens and young adults alike. Many reach this point because they feel helpless and do not know how to begin to address their overwhelming feelings. As school counselors, it is our job to help teens (along with their parents or guardians) make a support plan to guide them during this crucial time in their lives.

We can help teach staff, parents and other students how to recognize the warning signs of potential suicide. We can create opportunities to help connect students in need to resources that will help them.

In Olivia's case, I would help her and her parents connect with an outside agency that specializes in helping teens with suicidal thoughts. I would also schedule extra check-in times to see her and watch how things are progressing over the next few weeks.

When speaking to students about self-harm or suicide, it can be a very delicate conversation. More often than not, teenagers will be reluctant to share their inner feelings or thoughts, especially when they are speaking to an adult they do not trust. To build rapport with teens, be proactive. Become visible, available and persistent. Let them know that they are not alone. It is our job to listen to them, to see them, and to understand what they are going through.

According to the American School Counselor Association (ASCA) 2022 guidelines, mandated reporters do not need certainty, but only the notion of potential suicide to begin the process of support. Parents or guardians should be notified immediately upon learning of the possibility of a student's suicidal thoughts or intentions.

Offer the family resources. Make recommendations for outside agencies. If a family does not take a potential threat seriously, you may even need to file a report with Child Protective Services (CPS).

As counselors, we should train teachers and all staff to slow down and really see those teens in need. We all need to recognize teens' signals for help. Note changes in behavior, sudden lack of grooming, withdrawal, and other signals. Be compassionate in helping them through their struggles when they reach out.

If you or someone you know is experiencing self-harm or suicidal thoughts, please get help. Call: 988

~ OR ~

Call the National Suicide Hotline: 1-800-273-8255 (TALK)

OLIVIA'S OUTCOME:

Olivia's need to be seen and loved spiraled into a plan to completely change herself. When that didn't work, it morphed into a plan to end her life. Her emptiness had become too great to handle on her own, and she didn't trust that anyone could help her.

On the day that she planned to leave this world, a teacher heroically stepped in. Mr. Billings couldn't stop all her pain, but his actions sparked a flicker of trust that the counselor and Olivia's mom could then build upon to show Olivia how much she was loved and needed in this world.

The school counselor called Olivia's mom and explained that Olivia had been a victim of cyberbullying, which is a crime. They told her that Olivia was possibly going through depression and was at high-risk for suicide.

Olivia's mom realized how dire Olivia's situation was. She discovered just how close Olivia had been to following through on a suicide plan for herself. This made it clear to her that Olivia was not "going through a stage" or "being a dramatic teenager." Her mom could see that Olivia was, in fact, hurting and felt very unloved to the point where she felt she didn't matter to anyone in the world and wanted to leave it.

Olivia's mom started taking Olivia to a therapist. She learned to listen and empathize with her daughter more instead of just dismissing her thoughts and feelings. This allowed them to grow a bond and become closer to each other.

Through therapy, Olivia realized that the "naked" picture of her did not define her or her life. Yes, it was extremely traumatizing at the time. In fact, it was as close to a 10 as she had ever experienced up to that point in her life, almost as bad as when her dad had left.

But that picture did NOT define her. The trauma of experiencing cyberbullying could be overcome, and the perpetrator could be held accountable for her criminal actions.

Olivia is currently attending a four-year college studying social work. She wants to help teens who are afraid to trust and reach out for help because she knows sometimes that's the hardest step.

Especially when you don't trust that you'll get help.

Olivia learned that she could trust again, and the same goes for you, dear reader. Always remember that life gets better. It is always darkest before the dawn. Reach out for help when you need it, and keep asking until they hear you.

Final thoughts

There are two lessons I hope you've learned from reading this book. The first is that you have something to offer the world, but if you don't have a goal in mind, you will float. It's important to dream and to have some goals. If you are not working *towards* something, you are floating.

When you float through life, you change with the wind and become a "people pleaser." You don't know who you are, what you believe in, and you lose the ability to stand firm in your core values. When you float, you sit back and accept what happens to you in life. You get stuck.

The second lesson is that everyone in life struggles with something. Some just hide it better.

In your invisible backpack of life, you have all these boxes with issues in them, all competing with your thoughts, all wanting to grow and get bigger. They want to get so big that they derail you from your goals. Problems never go away. However, as a teen with tenacity, you've learned some skills to keep these issues (and the thoughts about them) small, so they don't overpower you and take you off your path.

You may be wondering which issues will get bigger and take you away from your goals.

The answer is, **"The ones you feed."**

TALE OF THE TWO WOLVES

A young boy came to his grandfather, filled with anger at another boy who had done him an injustice.

The old grandfather said to his grandson, "Let me tell you a story. I too, at times, have felt a great hate for those that have taken so much, with no sorrow for what they do.

"But hate wears you down, and hate does not hurt your enemy. Hate is like taking poison and wishing your enemy would die. I have struggled with these feelings many times.

"It is as if there are two wolves inside me.

"One wolf is good and does no harm. He lives in harmony with all around him and does not take offence when no offence was intended. He will only fight when it is right to do so, and in the right way.

"But the other wolf," the boy's grandfather warned, "is full of anger. The littlest thing will set him into a fit of temper. He fights everyone, all the time, for no reason. He cannot think because his anger and hate are so great. It is helpless anger because his anger will change nothing.

"Sometimes it is hard to live with these two wolves inside me, because both of the wolves try to dominate my spirit."

The boy looked intently into his grandfather's eyes and asked, "Which wolf will win, Grandfather?"

The grandfather smiled and said, *"The one I feed."*

The story of the two wolves, often referred to as "The One You Feed," is a Native American parable. It is commonly attributed to the Cherokee tribe, but its exact origins and specific tribe are debated.

The most crucial lesson hidden in the Native American story of the two wolves is this fact: **You have more power over your life than you think you do.**

In this world, it's easy to get beaten down by your circumstances, especially when they're not what you expected.

No matter who you are or where you come from, you have probably faced obstacles in life, and there will be many more.

As a teen with tenacity, you can use your skills to help you pursue your goals. The more you focus on your goals, the less room there will be for all the negative feelings that feed those issues in your backpack.

Have tenacity because this world needs you and YOU MATTER.

The End

~ Resources ~

Suicide and Crisis Lifeline:

988LIFELINE.ORG

Or call:

988

~

The National Suicide Hotline:

1-800-273-8255 (TALK)

~ Acknowledgements ~

To my spouse Alfred, my high-school sweetheart. You demonstrated your tenacity for 41 years when going to work every day and coming home to our family. Your constant love and support mean everything to me. I've loved you for 48 years and look forward to many more.

To my four children, Jackie, Chris, Nick and Eric, who proved how far tenacity can take you. I admire the grace and tenacity you've each shown during the years of struggles you have faced (Tourette's Syndrome, OCD, Dyslexia, ADD).

To my parents, Frank and Diane Keller, for instilling tenacity in me all those years ago. You had faith in me and gave me a great example of what tenacity looks like in your 68-year marriage.

To Dr. Scott Poland, my friend and suicidology expert. Thank you for providing the forward to my book. Let us relentlessly keep up the fight to protect our teens.

To Carrie Glenn, the best editor and author-coach imaginable. You took my thoughts and helped me create a strong message for teens who need skills to develop tenacity.

To Mindy Espinoza at Mindyedits@gmail.com. Your creativity on the book cover is amazing.

To The Metropolitan Museum of Art. Key photo credit: The Metropolitan Museum of Art, 1922. Title: Key. This Spanish, 16th century key runs 4¼ inches (10.8 cm) and is made of iron. Its credited line is "Gift of Henry G. Marquand, 1887." Accession number: 87.11.78. Provenance: Henry G. Marquand (until 1887; to MMA). Thank you for the image of the key via Open Access public domain:

https://www.metmuseum.org/art/collection/search/186858.

~ About the Authors ~

Kathy Espinoza has raised four children with learning disabilities, which include Tourette's Syndrome, OCD, Dyslexia and ADD. Learning the hard way that not all children are born "perfect," she worked hard to build tenacity in each of them, so they could become the best THEY could be. For the past 10 years, Kathy has worked with middle and high school students, offering them a "Teens with Tenacity" program to inspire first-generation Achievement Via Individual Determination (AVID) students to set goals, dream big and develop tenacity skills. Kathy's program helps teens learn to cope with the pressures of social media, bullying, gangs, teen drama, death and suicide ideation by learning age-appropriate stress management and time management techniques.

Jacquelyn (Jackie) Rathbun is a high school English teacher working with students from underserved populations in Southern California. She has been an educator for over 15 years, teaching at the elementary, middle school and high school levels. She has been an AVID co-coordinator at her current school, helping students reach their goals of higher education after high school. To also help her school's freshmen classes achieve higher pass rates, she has worked with the Building Assets Reducing Risks (BARR) program. Ms. Rathbun's greatest goal is to help students reach their full potential and to become the best versions of themselves.

Christopher Espinoza has served students as a school counselor for over 10 years. His focus has been addressing students through social emotional learning and personalized instruction to transform the learning potential of marginalized students' intellect and character. He is currently an Assistant Principal building relationships to foster teacher growth, maintain high instructional expectations, establish positive school culture and achieve excellence in student support. He encourages open lines of communication that support students with academic growth, social emotional learning and positive discipline strategies.

www.ingramcontent.com/pod-product-compliance
Lightning Source LLC
Chambersburg PA
CBHW080842120626
46553CB00009B/2532